Following Historic Trails

Travellers to the Mississippi

Philomena Hauck

Detselig Enterprises Ltd.
Calgary, Alberta

Following Historic Trails

Travellers to the Mississippi

Canadian Cataloguing in Publication Data

Hauck, Philomena, 1927-
    Travellers to the Mississippi

    (Following historic trails)
    Bibliography: p.
    ISBN 0-920490-98-0

    1. Mississippi River – Discovery and exploration
– Juvenile literature. I. Title. II Series.
F352.H38 1989   j977'.01   C89-091205-X

© 1989 by Detselig Enterprises Limited
P.O. Box G 399
Calgary, Alberta T3A 2G3

Printed in Canada   SAN 115-0324   ISBN 0-920490-98-0

Contents

Detselig Enterprises Ltd. appreciates the financial
assistance for its 1989 publishing program from

Alberta Foundation for the Literary Arts
Canada Council
Department of Communications
Alberta Culture

Introduction

Early French explorers in Canada heard tales from the native people about a mysterious river far in the west. The Algonkians called it the "Messippi," other tribes gave it different names, but, by all accounts, it was a great river, "the father of waters." Nobody knew the course of the river. According to one popular account, the Mississippi arose in a great mountain range spanning the centre of the continent and emptied itself into the western sea, or the Hudson Bay. If this was true, it could provide a safe water route to China and the riches of the Orient.

The first European to set eyes on the Mississippi was the Spanish explorer, Hernandez De Soto. The Spaniards were not greatly impressed by the discovery. They had come to North America in search of rich lands and precious metals, and the river was little more than an obstacle. For three years De Soto and his followers marched through muddy swamps and tangled undergrowth, but they found no treasure trove. Worn out by hunger and disease and under constant attack by Indian tribes, the wretched men groped their way to the Gulf of Mexico. In 1524, De Soto himself perished of yellow fever by the muddy waters of the great river and the remnants of his tattered army sailed back to Spain.

Apart from setting up a few trading posts, which gradually fell into decay, the Spaniards paid scant attention to the "Rio Grande" as they called the mighty river. Instead, they concentrated their attention on their older colonies in Mexico and South America where there was gold and treasure in abundance.

Almost a century passed by before another explorer attempted to reach the Mississippi, this time from the north. There was no permanent French settlement in Canada until 1618, although Jacques Cartier made the first of his famous voyages to Quebec in 1534. Cartier's objectives were to search for precious metals and to seek out the fabled route to China. The "gold" he found turned out to be iron pyrites, no route to China was

1

discovered, and the few settlers who managed to survive the terrible scurvy and the harsh winter packed up and sailed for France.

Years rolled by before France made another attempt to settle the New World. Racked by civil war at home, the country had no resources for foreign exploration. Yet, of their own accord, hardy fishermen from French ports braved the Atlantic gales to reach the teeming fishing grounds off the coast of Newfoundland and returned to France with their rich hauls. Frequently, the fishermen ventured ashore to barter knives, kettles and trinkets in return for bear and beaver skins from the native people. The lure of the riches to be made from the fur trade spurred the French king to develop Cartier's former colony. If the explorers could also find the elusive gold and water route to China, so much the better.

The greatest explorer of all was Samuel de Champlain. On one of his numerous voyages of discovery, he ascended the Ottawa River, pushed on to Lake Nipissing, then turned southward until he reached the shores of Georgian Bay. Native tribes from the area regaled him with tales of a great river that flowed west into a far-off sea. From their information, he traced the possible course of the river on his map and he allowed himself to hope that the remote river flowed into the China Sea.

With Champlain, to think was to act. He settled on a voyageur named Jean Nicollet –
a man who had spent several years in the country of the Nipissings and knew their language. In the summer of 1634, Nicollet paddled up the Ottawa River in a birch-bark canoe on the first stage of his journey. In case he should meet Chinese mandarins, he bought along a damask robe strewn with flowers and birds of many colors. Nicollet never actually reached the Mississippi, although he came close to one of its tributaries, the Wisconsin.

For 35 years, the river was to remain a mystery. Samuel de Champlain was dead and there was nobody with his vision to replace him. Moreover, the infant colony was locked in almost continuous wars with the Iroquois, its outposts were destroyed, and the inhabitants lived in daily fear of their lives.

After the defeat of the Iroquois, the French turned their minds once more to exploration. By then, fur traders and Jesuit priests who penetrated deeper and deeper into the wilderness had collected more reports about the great river. Some people guessed that De Soto's "Rio Grande" and the Mississippi were one and the same. Others clung to the notion that the river flowed into the Vermilion Sea (the Gulf of California).

The great Intendant Jean Talon decided to settle the question. Talon had ambitious plans for New France. He aimed to improve trade and agriculture as well as extending French influence all across the continent. He looked about him for a man capable of exploring the Mississippi and his choice fell on Louis Jolliet, a Canadian-born fur trader. A Jesuit priest named Father Jacques Marquette who knew several native languages was chosen to accompany him to preach the gospel to any Indian tribes they might meet along the way.

In May 1673 the two men, accompanied by five native guides, set off on their memorable journey. In their light birch-bark canoe, they maneuvered their way through rivers and lakes for about a month until the broad Mississippi came into view. After paddling down the river as far as De Soto's last resting place, they turned for home. To go any farther was hazardous. The guns and utensils in the hands of the native people told them that the Spaniards had been there, so the journey could cost the explorers their lives. Although they had not traced the great river to its mouth, Jolliet and Marquette had settled one burning question: the Mississippi flowed south toward the Gulf of Mexico.

On the homeward voyage, Jolliet's canoe overturned in the Lachine rapids and all his maps and records were lost, so we have no official version of the journey except the one which he later wrote from memory. An account based on Father Marquette's journal still survives, but the priest was a poor cartographer and he also omitted several details, which were probably buried with Jolliet's records.

The news of the discovery created little stir in Quebec. There were no maps or charts to show the course of the river and no stories of daring deeds or hairbreadth escapes. Besides, it was disappointing to learn that the Mississippi did not empty itself into the western sea. Many years passed by before the two brave and modest men received the credit they deserved. Their fame was over shadowed by that of explorer Robert Cavelier de la Salle.

Before Marquette and Jolliet discovered the Mississippi, La Salle had made some discoveries of his own. Leaving his home in Fort Frontenac on the northern shore of Lake Ontario, he wandered alone through the dense forests gathering information about the wilderness to the south and west. In his journeying, he explored the rivers and streams, mapped out the trails and discovered the Ohio, which the native people called the "Beautiful River." In 1675, he crossed the sea to France and laid an ambitious scheme before the French King, Louis XIV. The plan was not merely to find the mouth of the Mississippi, but to set up a huge industrial and commercial colony between Quebec and Mexico.

In Paris, he found a young soldier named Henry de Tonty whom he chose as his agent and lieutenant. La Salle chose better than he knew. Of all his followers, Tonty was to be the most faithful and courageous and he had more than his fair share of adventures himself. Besides Tonty, another conspicuous member of the expedition was

Father Louis Hennepin, a Recollet (Francisan) priest. Father Hennepin did some exploring of his own on the Upper Mississippi and his books about his real and imaginary adventures created a sensation in France.

With the King's patent in his pocket, La Salle and his men set out from Lake Ontario on August 7, 1679. After incredible hardships and delays, his expedition managed to trace the Mississippi to the coast. Finally, on April 9, 1682, he stood on the sandy shore and claimed the river, all its tributaries and surrounding lands for the King of France. The Mississippi land had finally yielded its secrets.

After his discovery, La Salle was not content to rest on his laurels. Leaving Tonty in charge of the projected new colony on the banks of the Illinois River, he went to France with a new proposal. This time his objective was to sail from France to the Mississippi delta and set up a colony from which an attack could be mounted against the Spaniards in New Mexico. With luck, the French would gain control over the whole river and drive the Spaniards out of North America.

With the King's consent, La Salle set out on his ill-fated voyage in 1684. Because of a navigational error, his ships overshot the delta by more than 400 miles and ended up in Matagorda Bay in the present state of Texas. Weeks and months went by in a futile search for the fatal river. At length he lost hope. Leaving some of his followers in a ramshackle fort near the bay, he struck out for help with his ablest men on the long trek to Tonty's fort in Illinois country. On the way, he was murdered by one of his own men, his body left to the beasts of the field.

When news of La Salle's death reached Tonty, he set out, with a few followers, for the Texas wilderness in an effort to find the explorer's followers marooned in the fort. After a long and painful journey, his guides abandoned him and he was forced to turn back.

Twelve years after La Salle's death another gallant Canadian, Pierre Le Moyne D'Iberville founded the colony of Louisiana on lands claimed by La Salle. Later the French set up a line of forts from the falls of St. Anthony (near the present Minneapolis, St. Paul), first discovered by Father Hennepin, all the way to New Orleans. For a time it looked as though New France would control the river and control the continent. But the battle of the Plains of Abraham put an end to French dominance and the mighty Mississippi passed into British, and later, American hands.

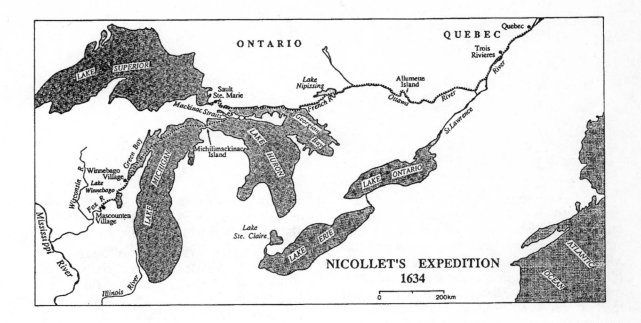

NICOLLET'S EXPEDITION
1634

Chapter One

Jean Nicollet

In the summer of 1634, a frail birch bark canoe carrying a Frenchman and seven Huron companions paddled down the straits separating Lake Huron from Lake Michigan. The lone Frenchman was Jean Nicollet, the first European ever to pass that way. On his adventurous voyage, he hoped to discover the Mississippi River with the added prospect that the river might prove to be a safe water route to China.

Jean Nicollet arrived in Canada when he was 20-years-old. He had come from the coastal town of Cherbourg, Normandy, where his father was a postal courier. As a young boy, Jean probably heard stories about the teeming fishing grounds and the rich fur-trading lands of New France from the sailors who risked their lives on the treacherous Atlantic waves to reach the new country. Jean imagined a huge country peopled by strange tribes, and a life full of wonders and excitement. His dream of adventure became a reality in 1618 when he met the great explorer, Samuel de Champlain, who invited him to come to Canada.

Champlain was in Cherbourg waiting for his ship to be loaded for the voyage back to the new colony. Ten years earlier, he had founded the little settlement of Quebec. He envisioned a colony that would be more than a collection of trading posts – it would be a great country with a permanent population. Like many people of his day, he believed that the new land's western flowing rivers would provide a short and easy passage to China. Champlain believed that one day the European ships would no longer sail to the Orient by the long and dangerous, southern route through the Straits of Magellan, but would use the great rivers of Canada.

To achieve his dream, Champlain needed money and people. Above all, he needed able young men like Nicollet who were willing to live among the native people, learn their language and keep them on friendly terms with the French. Champlain had reason to be pleased with his latest recruit. According to those who knew him, the young Norman was brave, intelligent and posessed an excellent memory.

Nicollet arrived in Quebec in June 1618. As the boat sailed under the towering rock, he saw Champlain's little "habitation" on the river bank. It consisted of a few buildings, a storehouse protected by deep ditches, an open space and a few small vegetable gardens. The only real settlers in the whole colony were Louis Hébert and his family. Of the other fifty Frenchmen, four were Recollet (Franciscan) priests and the remaining forty-six were fur traders.

The tents of the Montagnais Indians were clustered near the French settlement. While the Montagnais men were fishing for eel in the St. Lawrence River, the women sat on the shore mending the fishing nets or tending to their pots of sagamite. Old men sat around the fires gravely smoking their pipes and the children played freely nearby.

Nicollet remained in Quebec for a few months. His real work began as winter approached and Champlain sent the young man to Alumette Island to live with the Algonkin Indians. The island was 200 miles south of Quebec on the Ottawa River. The position of the island was strategic because it was on the Hurons' fur-trading path to Quebec. Consequently, it was important for the French to keep on friendly terms with the Algonkins so that the Hurons would be allowed to pass the island in peace.

The Algonkins were a nomadic tribe who followed the fish in the summer and the game in the winter. Nicollet lived among them for two years and shared their way of life. He wore the same clothes, ate the same food and went hungry when food ran out. One winter, food was so scarce that he lived for seven weeks on fish bones and tree bark. In summer, he was plagued by the mosquitoes which a Frenchman once described as being worse than wolves. (The Indians greased their bodies to protect them against mosquitoes and flies.)

There were good times too. He enjoyed the singing, dancing and storytelling, and he admired the people's generosity to him and to each other. Before long, they adopted him as a son and even made him a chief. On one occasion, he accompanied them to a Mohawk village where he helped to make peace between the two tribes who had been warring for years.

After two years on the island without seeing a fellow countryman, Nicollet returned to Quebec. He was toughened by life in the wilderness, and he spoke the Huron and Algonkian languages like a native. After his years in the wilderness, he enjoyed the comforts of the settlement where he could sleep in a real bed, eat tasty French bread and go to Mass and confession.

Nicollet did not enjoy these comforts for long. In a few months Champlain sent him on another mission, this time to stay with the Nipissing Indians about 200 miles farther west. Nicollet built a cabin close to the Nipissing village and lived with them for nine years. He hunted and fished, did some fur-trading, and taught the natives how to use the needle and the awl to sew and make holes in the animal skins. The natives gave him the Indian name "Achirra," and invited him to all their council meetings.

As a result of his long sojourn, living as an Indian among Indians and his inability to attend to his religious duties, Nicollet began to worry about losing his soul. Although he had a few holy books among his scanty possessions, he had not seen a priest for nine years; it was time to leave his native friends and return to Quebec. On his arrival in the settlement, he made his way to the church where he said his prayers and lit a votive candle.

Nicollet barely had time to rest from the journey before a catastrophe hit Quebec. An English ship commanded by David Kirke sailed up the St. Lawrence River and demanded the surrender of the fort. After holding out as long as he could, Champlain knew that further opposition was useless. There were only 50 men in the fort who could bear arms, and hardly any gunpowder. Only 10 pounds of flour were left to feed the starving people.

During the three years of British control,

Nicollet lived among his Huron friends and prevented them from trading with the conquerors. After Champlain returned to power, Nicollet asked for, and received the position of clerk in the Company of One Hundred Associates at Trois-Rivières.

Ever the explorer, Champlain still had visions of discovering the short route to China. The Hurons had told him about a tribe called the "Gens de Mer" who lived on the shores of a great sea and traded with another more distant people. Nicollet, too, had heard stories about far-off tribes without hair or beards. Could these people be Chinese? The only way to find out was to send an explorer deep into the west.

Nicollet was the ideal choice; his years with the Algonkins and the Nipissings had taught him how to survive in the wilderness and how to speak the native languages. Indeed, one objective of the voyage was to visit the Winnebagos, an Algonkian tribe who lived near present-day Green Bay, and urge them to make peace with their other Algonkian neighbors. To prepare himself for a possible meeting with the Chinese, Nicollet obtained a golden damask robe embroidered with birds and flowers.

On July 1, 1634, Nicollet set out on his momentous journey. On his way, he stopped off at Trois-Rivières to help lay down stakes for a future settlement. He then joined a fleet of canoes under the leadership of Father Jean de Brébeuf, who was on his way to preach the gospel to the Hurons. After parting with Father de Brébeuf at Allumette Island, Nicollet continued past thundering waterfalls to Lake Nipissing. The canoes often had to be carried over shallow portages, and the sharp stones in the river bed cut into the men's feet.

COURRIER DU BOIS.

Illustration by Frederic Remington. © Glenbow Archives NA-1406-55.

After a brief rest with the friendly Nipissings, Nicollet paddled across the lake and followed the French River which pours into Georgian Bay. Hugging the northern shores of Lake Huron, he reached the Huron village of Sault Ste. Marie where he rested and recruited seven Huron guides.

Nicollet and his guides followed the Saint Mary River south toward Michilimackinac (now known as Mackinac). Straight ahead was the large turtle-shaped island which the Indians also called Michilimackinac. With its white limestone cliffs soaring above forests of pine, spruce and tamarack, the island had a mysterious beauty and was considered to be a Huron holy place. As they passed close to the shore, the Huron boatmen threw pieces of tobacco into the waters to appease their manitou or Great Spirit. It is not known if Nicollet ever stopped on the island, but today a plaque with the words "Nicollet's Watchtower" is on the side of a tall cliff by the shore.

As the island receded into the distance, the canoe slipped along a lake never previously penetrated by a European. Today it is known as Lake Michigan, but Nicollet called it "The Second Lake of the Hurons." After paddling along the eastern side of the lake for about a week, the men saw clouds of blue smoke in the distance. They were nearing the home of the Winnebagos.

Donning his golden robe and taking a pistol in each hand, Nicollet stepped from his canoe and entered the village. The villagers feared the strange white man in the long bright garment. Cautiously at first, a few of the bolder men inched forward to peer at him. As they advanced, Nicollet fired two shots into the air, and the natives scattered in all directions. Unused to firearms, they thought Nicollet must be a god who could fire thunder into the air.

As news of his arrival spread through the village of 4 000 to 5 000 people, the chiefs turned out to greet the stranger. The peace pipe was passed and a feast of 120 beavers was prepared in his honor. Nicollet told them about the King of France and about the trade goods they could expect if they became allies of the French and made peace with their own neighbors. After listening carefully to Nicollet's speech, the chiefs readily agreed to make peace.

The first part of his mission was accomplished, but where was the river leading to the China Sea? The Winnebagos told him about other large tribes and great western-flowing rivers. Nicollet decided to seek these rivers out. He paddled south on the Fox River until he reached the village of the Muscoutens, another Algonkian tribe. They also held a feast in his honor and told him that he was only a few days' journey from a river that flowed into a great water. The river was the Wisconsin and the great water was the Mississippi, not the sea as Nicollet thought.

Nicollet veered south toward the Illinois River, also a tributary of the Mississippi, but as the cold weather approached he decided to turn back. He spent the winter comfortably with the Potawatomi Indians while the biting wind and heavy snow gripped the Wisconsin woods. He had not reached the great river which was supposed to lead to China, but he had penetrated far into hitherto unknown land.

As soon as the rivers were clear of ice, Nicollet and his faithful Huron guides returned the way they had come. At Lake Nipissing he joined a group of Hurons on their way to Quebec. He arrived in the fall of 1635, just before the last ship of the year set sail for France.

No bells were tolled to mark Nicollet's return, but one man eagerly listened to his story – Samuel de Champlain. Ill though he was, Champlain wrote a report to the French king urging him to send over some soldiers to extend French rule over the whole continent. It was the last letter Champlain ever wrote, for he died on Christmas day of the same year.

Meanwhile, Nicollet set out for Trois-Rivières to work as a clerk and interpreter. It was a responsible job: he selected and ordered trade goods from France, placed them in the store, and later exchanged the goods for furs, which he then packed and exported.

After he settled into his new job, he was married to Margaret Couillard, the grand-daughter of Louis Hébert, the first Canadian settler, and the young couple had a son and a daughter. Nicollet's wandering days were over. With his brother-in-law, he obtained two grants of land, one in Trois-Rivières and one on the Plains of Abraham. More a trader than a farmer, he spent the greater part of his time in the fur-trading store. He was an important man in the colony, well-respected by settlers and natives alike. In his spare time, he acted as interpreter to the new missionaries in the colony and he took great pleasure in teaching the native children about the Christian religion.

Nicollet's good fortune did not last long. The fall of 1642, he was in Quebec when news reached him that the Hurons at Trois-Rivières had captured, and were about to kill a chief from another tribe. Such an act would likely cause a tribal war which would affect the whole colony. The only person with enough influence over the Hurons to prevent the killing was Jean Nicollet.

On a cold and stormy evening in October, Nicollet set out for Trois-Rivières to try to settle the dispute. The frail canoe Nicollet was travelling in capsized in the icy waters of the St. Lawrence River near Sillery. Unable to swim, he held on to the canoe as long as he could. Knowing he no longer had the strength to hold on, he called to his companion: "Goodbye de Chavigny, make for the shore, you can swim. I am going to God. Be good to my wife and children." Then all was over.

Nicollet's body was never recovered. The settlers mourned his death. The Indians, too, had lost a good friend and it is said that they went down to the shore crying "Art thou gone Achirra and will we never see you again?" The Hurons released their prisoner, sent him back to his own tribe, and peace was maintained. Nicollet would have been glad to know his death was not in vain.

Champlain was dead, Nicollet was dead and his voyage all but forgotten. It was 35 years before another Frenchman made his way toward the Mississippi River. That man was Louis Jolliet, a nephew of Jean Nicollet.

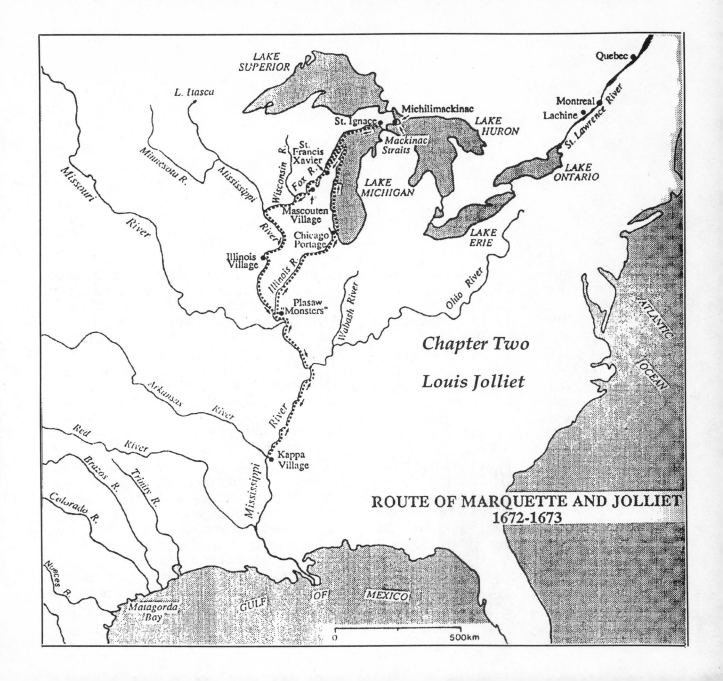

LAKE SUPERIOR

L. Itasca

Quebec

Montreal
Lachine

St. Lawrence River

Michilimackinac

St. Ignace

Minnesota R.

Mississippi

St. Francis Xavier

Wisconsin R.

Fox R.

Mackinac Straits

LAKE HURON

Missouri River

Mascouten Village

LAKE MICHIGAN

LAKE ONTARIO

Chicago Portage

LAKE ERIE

Illinois Village

Illinois R.

Plasaw "Monsters"

Wabash River

Ohio River

Mississippi River

ATLANTIC OCEAN

Arkansas River

Chapter Two

Louis Jolliet

Red River

Brazos R.

Trinity R.

Kappa Village

Colorado R.

Mississippi

Nueces R.

ROUTE OF MARQUETTE AND JOLLIET 1672-1673

Matagorda Bay

GULF OF MEXICO

0   500km

On a house in Lower Town, Quebec City, there is a plaque bearing the name of Louis Jolliet. The plaque commemorates the birthplace of the first North American-born explorer to reach the Mississippi River.

Jolliet was baptized on September 21, 1645 in the Church of the Immaculate Conception in Quebec. He was the second son of wagon maker, Jean Jolliet, and his wife, Marie D'Abancourt. The Jolliet family lived in a little log house by the bank of the mighty St. Lawrence. Behind the house, the steep Rue de Montagne wound its way to the Governor's residence which was perched on the great rock overlooking the Fort St. Louis harbor. A few scattered houses lined the narrow street but most of Quebec's 200 people had their homes by the shore in Lower Town.

Young Jolliet grew up in difficult times. In 1648, the Iroquois destroyed the whole Huron nation and made themselves masters of the river. The fur trade was in ruins, and as furs were the livelihood of the colony, the settlers spoke of returning to France. Without furs, the settlers could not afford to buy the provisions and tools they needed. The Jolliet family had their own troubles. Jean died in 1651, leaving a wife and four children to fend for themselves. But, life had to go on. The widow, Marie D'Abancourt, took up the threads of her life and married Geoffrey Guillot, a nearby settler, the following year.

Young Louis went to school at the Jesuit college, and at the age of 17, he made up his mind to become a priest. It was customary for the college students to debate their philosophy course subject in front of an audience. Jolliet argued his case well, before a group that included Governor Courcelle, Intendant Talon and Bishop Laval. He was a good student whose interests extended to music and he sometimes played the organ in the cathedral.

When he was 22, Jolliet decided he was not cut-out to be a priest and he received permission to leave the seminary. With the help of a loan from Bishop Laval, the young man left for France. Some people say that Talon encouraged Jolliet to go to France, so that he could learn more about map-making and waterways. If Talon had his eye on the young man, his confidence was well-founded.

Louis returned to Quebec the following year. He bought kettles, hatchets, tobacco and other goods that the native people liked from a Quebec merchant, and to all appearances, he planned to become a fur trader. Jolliet vanished for a few years, only to appear in 1671 at the village of Sault Ste. Marie. That year Daumont de Lausson, a fellow explorer, took possession of the area in the name of France. A great throng of native people gathered to witness the ceremony. Then the ambassadors from the tribes affixed their signs to a great parchment. Beside the native totems – the beaver, the fish, the fox, the deer, the eagle and the moose antlers – were the French signatures which included that of Louis Jolliet, fur trader.

It was Intendant Talon who planned the expedition to Sault Ste. Marie. Although the great Intendant knew the importance of agriculture, he wanted to explore and discover new territories for France. Ever since Champlain's time, people knew about the great Mississippi River; however, it was one thing to know it existed, it was another thing to find it. Talon wanted to settle the question once and for all, and he chose Jolliet for the job.

When Frontenac arrived in Canada in 1672, Talon put the plan before him. Nothing could have pleased the new governor more. He fell in with the plan at once and wrote enthusiastically to France saying: "The Sieur Jolliet is very skillful in those kinds of discoveries and has already been near the great river. . . . We shall have certain news of it this summer. . . . " No mean explorers themselves, the Jesuits also backed Jolliet: "He has both tact and prudence, which are the chief characteristics required for the success of a voyage as dangerous as it is difficult. He has the courage to dread nothing where everything is to be feared."

Jolliet had the approval, now he had to find the money. There was nothing to be had from the government. If Jolliet wanted to go on the expedition he would have to finance it himself. With his brother, Zacharie, and six other men, he set up a fur-trading company whose profits were to be used for the venture.

The ink was scarcely dry on the new contract when Jolliet left Quebec. With a squad of crewmen he set off for the Jesuit mission at St. Ignace in Michlimackinac. There he was to deliver a letter from Father Dablon, the Superior of the Jesuits to Father Marquette. The letter contained an order for

Marquette to accompany Jolliet on his travels. On December 8, 1672 Jolliet arrived at the little pallisaded mission house at St. Ignace and presented Father Dablon's message.

Father Marquette was delighted with the news. All his life he had longed to explore far-off lands and to preach the gospel to tribes who had never seen a priest before. That winter the two men prepared for the voyage. Jolliet talked to the native people about the streams, lakes and rivers, and he managed to make a rough map of the Mississippi.

Shooting the Rapids
Reprinted, by permission, National Archives of Canada: C2774.

Toward the middle of May, they set out on their memorable journey. It was a small party, only seven people, for such a bold undertaking. Two birch-bark canoes carried the men and all their belongings – ammunition, gifts for the native people, maps, food and other supplies. The food was simple: a few sacks of Indian corn and some smoked meat. On the river, two men paddled each canoe while the third man rested. Father Marquette was free to observe the countryside and make notes in his journal.

The native people lined the shore to bid farewell to the seven adventurers. For five days the canoes coasted along the shores of Lake Michigan. It was beautiful spring weather, the sun glistened on the calm waters of the lake and the trees that lined the margin were bursting into full leaf. By day they paddled merrily along and when night approached they beached their canoes, lit a fire and sat down for their evening meal. Their first stop was the village of the Menominee Indians near Green Bay.

The Menominee were a peaceful nation whom the French had christened "La Nation de Folle-Avoine," or "Wild Rice Indians." The name came from the wild rice that grew in the marshes and lakes that dotted the area. On their arrival in the village, Jolliet and his men were warmly greeted and treated to a meal of wild rice "almost as good as rice where no seasoning is added."

Except for the meal, the Wild Rice people had little comfort for the travellers. When told of the proposed journey to the

Mississippi, the chiefs did their best to get their visitors to turn back. They warned them about savage tribes who lived only to kill and who could stop a charging buffalo by grasping its horns. They told of the ravenous monsters of the river who could devour the travellers and their canoes at one gulp. As if these stories were not enough, they went on to warn about the fierce heats and terrible rapids facing the unsuspecting traveller. Many of the stories the chiefs told were quite true, but the explorers, who knew nothing about alligators or tropical heat, continued blithely on their journey.

The explorers next came to the mission of St. Francis Xavier at the head of Green Bay, where they were welcomed by the Jesuit priest Fr. Claude Allouez. After a brief stop for fresh supplies, they paddled up the Fox River, which was bounded on each side by green meadows and tall trees. At one point where the river narrowed, they saw a few fishermen casting their nets into the water. The timid natives, the last of the once powerful Petun tribe, cautiously approached the canoes with a gift of fresh fish.

Farther upstream, the explorers came face to face with a series of rapids. As the rapids became more and more violent, the men were forced to disembark from their canoes and carry them on their weary shoulders. At the entrance to Lake Winnebago, the river widened to form a swamp. They manoeuvered the canoes with difficulty through the main channel until they reached the village of the Mascoutens, or Fire Nation. Perched on a hill overlooking a prairie dotted with vines and tobacco plants the village was a welcome sight. More welcome still was the sight of a cross surrounded by native offerings. Father Allouez had visited the village the previous year and the villagers still respected the Christian symbol.

Again, Jolliet and his men were given a hearty welcome. In the evening, the explorer spoke to the council of wise men, telling them about his journey and asked for guides to lead them to the Wisconsin River. The natives listened gravely to his speech and readily agreed to his request. Next morning, the men set out with two Miami guides and with a soft mat to ease the travellers' slumbers.

With the help of the guides, the canoes wormed their way through reeds and marshes. The next day they reached a portage leading to the Wisconsin. For one and a half miles, they carried their canoes across the soggy ground to the banks of the river. Bidding farewell to the trusty guides, Jolliet and his men launched the boats on the uncharted waters.

As they glided down the tranquil river, they admired the lush plains and dense woodlands spreading out before them. No human beings or smoke of an Indian village could be seen on the horizon. Timid deer and herds of wild buffalo grazed peacefully by the river bank, schools of fish danced in the water and flocks of birds flew overhead. Then on June 17, a low green island came into view, and beyond it the broad waters of the Mississippi. With joyful hearts, they gazed upon the "great river" and sang a hymn of thanksgiving.

Day after day they paddled cautiously down the winding river. In the evening, they would light a small fire to cook their simple meal, and when finished quench the flames and anchor farther ahead, leaving a man on watch in case of a surprise attack. After eight days, they saw human footmarks on the west shore. The men paused to decide on their next move. Jolliet knew Talon wanted information about the native tribes and about the direction of the Mississippi, so after discussion, he decided to take Father Marquette with him on the trail of the footmarks, leaving five voyageurs to guard the canoes.

The two men stole quietly along the trail, alert for the smallest rustle in the surrounding woods. In an hour, they came to a clearing. On a hill, stood an Indian village which was flanked by two other settlements. Not a soul saw their approach, until Jolliet stepped forward and announced his arrival in a loud voice. At the sound, the startled natives rushed out of the main village and stared at the two men, standing fearlessly before them. Then the natives, lead by four elders, approached the Blackrobe and his companion.

To their joy, the Frenchmen learned that they had reached an Illinois village. The Illinois, and their friends the Miami, belonged to the Algonkian nation whose language was known to Father Marquette. Greetings were exchanged and the visitors were escorted to the largest village. Some of the natives who had never before seen a white man ran ahead of the strangers to study them more closely. At the village, the peace pipe was passed around and Jolliet made a speech assuring the Miami of French support against the Iroquois enemy. This was good news to the Miami who had been driven from their former homeland by the Iroquois.

Indian with Pipe.
Reprinted from Du Creux, Francois, *Historiae Canadensis seu Novea Franciae*. Paris, 1664. Reprinted, by permission, National Archives of Canada: C99229.

After the speeches, the French were treated to a great feast, fed to them at the hands of the natives themselves. First came bowls of sagamite, followed by platters of boiled fish. The second course – an Indian delicacy, a boiled dog – was politely declined. The meal ended with a dish of buffalo meat. The following day, the chief presented Jolliet with a calumet (or peace pipe) to help secure a safe passage through the Indian nations. As a final gesture of friendship, the explorers were given an Indian boy to be their servant.

The explorers continued down the river, and within a few miles came upon a huge rock painted with multicolored grotesque monsters. Marquette noted: "They are as big as calves and have antlers like deer. Their faces are rather like the faces of men, with tigrous mouths and red eyes. Their bodies are covered with scales and their tails are so long that they pass over their heads and down between their legs, terminating like the tails of fishes. The colors used are red, green, and black."

Beyond the weird paintings, the turbulent Missouri River rushed violently into the Mississippi. The light canoes were flung like leaves in the wind. Tree trunks and shrubs were also hurled in the torrent, and a muddy avalanche darkened the blue water. Righting their canoes, the men paddled past the mouth of the Ohio River or "Beautiful River."

The perils of the torrent behind them, the men sweltered in the scorching heat. Even worse were the hordes of mosquitoes that swarmed around the canoes. With a piece of sail cloth over the boats to protect themselves from the voracious insects, the party paddled on. Near the present-day city of Memphis, Tennessee, Jolliet spied a group of Indians on the west shore. It was a perilous situation – seven men against twenty braves brandishing muskets and shouting wildly. Summoning all of his courage, Jolliet steered cautiously toward them while Marquette held the calumet high in the air. Recognizing the symbol, the native people invited the voyagers ashore and presented them with a feast of buffalo meat and wild plums. In halting Huron, they informed Jolliet that the mouth of the Mississippi could be reached in ten days. In fact, the river was still 1 000 miles distant.

Heartened by this news, Jolliet continued south. The explorers faced the worst threat so far at the junction of the St. Francis river in the present state of Arkansas. A crowd of warlike natives burst forth from their village, jumped into large wooden boats and attacked the two canoes. Clubs and arrows whizzed through the air, but Jolliet kept his nerve and ordered his men to hold their fire. He stood steadfastly in his canoe, while Father Marquette brandished the calumet. On the shore two chiefs saw the peace symbol and restrained the young braves. Not without some misgivings, Jolliet led his men ashore, where they were treated with the usual Indian hospitality.

With renewed hope, they set out the following morning accompanied by a native interpreter and an escort of ten men in a large canoe from a neighboring Arkansas village. A few miles downstream two canoes came out to meet them. In the village, they were seated on soft rush mats and presented with a feast of sagamite and corn, prepared in beautiful earthenware pots. From the assortment of hoes, beads, and hatchets in the village, it was obvious that the tribe had come in contact with earlier Spanish explorers. The chief warned Jolliet about warlike white men who spoke a different language and about warlike tribes armed with the white man's weapons. During the night, some of the young Arkansas braves plotted to kill the Frenchmen and steal their canoes, but the chief reprimanded them for such a breach of the laws of hospitality.

The next morning, Jolliet held a meeting with his men. Should they continue to the mouth of the Mississippi or return home? The prize was near, but the risks were enormous. One thing they knew for certain. The Mississippi flowed into the Gulf of Mexico, not the Pacific, as Talon had hoped. Rather than risking almost certain death at the hands of the Spaniards, or the hostile tribes, Jolliet decided to turn back. They were still about 700 miles from the sea, though the natives had led them to believe that the coast was much closer.

Paddling against the current, they wended their way north. On the way, they met friendly Illinois tribesmen who advised them to go by way of the Illinois River instead of taking the much longer route of the Wisconsin. Halfway up the river, a guide from one of the Illinois villages led them to the Chicago portage. At the end of the portage they launched their canoes on Lake Michigan and made their way safely to the Jesuit mission in Green Bay. In four months, they had travelled more than 2 500 miles, and without the loss of a single life or firing a single shot. They had traced the famous Mississippi for over 1 000 miles.

Jolliet spent the winter in Sault Ste. Marie working on his maps and completing his journal. In his spare moments he taught the young Indian servant how to read and write. In the spring, Jolliet set out for Quebec with three of his men and the young Indian boy. Wrapped carefully in the boat were his precious papers and samples of rocks, plants and calumets. Only 8 miles from home, near the Lachine rapids, a violent wave overturned the canoe, killing two boatmen and the Indian youth. Jolliet narrowly escaped with his life, but all his precious papers were lost. Even the copies he had left at Sault Ste. Marie were later burnt in a fire that swept through the mission house.

"Nothing remains to me but my life," he wrote to Frontenac. "I had escaped every danger. I had suffered no harm from Indians. I had passed many rapids. I was nearing home, full of the joy at the success of a long and difficult voyage. . . ." Jolliet grieved for the loss of the Indian boy. He described the boy to Bishop Laval: "He was 10 years old, quick-witted, diligent, obedient and endowed with an excellent disposition." The loss of Jolliet's papers was a great blow, not just to him, but to the world. All that remains to us are the reports which he wrote from memory and documents based on Marquette's diary.

Back in Quebec, Jolliet, now 30-years-old, made up his mind to settle down. His bride was Claire Francois Bissot, the 19-year-old daughter of a rich fur merchant. The following year he asked permission to form a settlement in the fertile Illinois country he had discovered. He was refused: "We must increase the number of settlers," the French minister wrote, "before thinking of other lands." With that, Jolliet had to be content. Together with a few partners, he turned his hand to fur-trading and seal fishing on the north shore of the St. Lawrence. He was an important man in the colony. When Frontenac called together 20 notables to discuss the thorny question of liquor sales to the native people, Jolliet was among those chosen. At the "Brandy Parliament," as the discussion was called, his view that liquor should be sold in the settlement but not in the wilderness was adopted.

The explorer was to make one more long journey, this time to the Hudson Bay. In the summer of 1679, Jolliet, his brother, Zacharie, and a small party of men set out on the 1 000 mile journey. His fame had preceded him. The commander of the bay, Charles Bayly, received him cordially and made him a handsome offer if he would join the English. Thanking him for his offer, Jolliet replied that he was born a Frenchman and would die a Frenchman. Back in Quebec, he made a report about the success of the English in the bay. He foresaw the ruin of the Canadian fur trade unless the English were dispossessed, or at least kept in check.

Meanwhile, Jolliet was rewarded with tracts of land. In 1679, he and a partner were granted the Mignan Islands in the St. Lawrence River. The following year he was granted the island of Anticosti. The island of more than one and a half million acres was surrounded by dangerous reefs and often shrouded by thick fog. Jolliet set up a large fishing trade and, on the north shore, he erected a home where he lived for the summer months with his wife and seven children. He became thoroughly familiar with the native ways and he always dealt fairly with them. During one of his frequent voyages, he also made a very useful chart of the St. Lawrence River for Governor Denonville.

For a few years, fortune smiled on Jolliet. He continued his fur-trading, and his fisheries provided the colony with most of its fish. However, events outside of his control conspired to ruin him. A fleet from New England, under the command of Sir William Phipps, sailed up the St. Lawrence in an attempt to capture Quebec. Jolliet's ship with his wife and mother-in-law on board was seized and the two women taken prisoner. The women were later released, but the valuable cargo of fish was confiscated. A further catastrophe followed. English ships bore down on Jolliet's forts on Anticosti and Mingan, ransacked all his goods and burned the buildings to the ground.

After all his efforts, Jolliet was a poor man. Far from conquered, he put forward a plan to explore the coast of Labrador, to open up trading with the local Indians and Inuit and to convert them. With the support of a rich Quebec merchant, Jolliet, a Recollet priest and 12 other men, set out for Labrador. For several days he explored the coast and made careful notes and drawings. One day he was amazed to see icebergs like tall castles in the distance. Hearing two loud reports like cannon shots, he sailed out to investigate. It was only the noise of icebergs breaking up and crashing into the sea.

On his voyage, Jolliet met Inuit and visited one of their villages. The Inuit were nervous at first, but as time went on, they plucked up courage and entertained their visitors with songs and dances. Jolliet noted that they were friendly, well-built people. At the end of August, he returned to Quebec and wrote an account of his journey. The account, with its many excellent maps, was very helpful to future travellers.

Late the following year, Jolliet was chosen to pilot a ship bound for France through the dangerous waters of the St. Lawrence. According to Governor Frontenac, Jolliet was the only man in the colony who could guide the ship between the ice floes. After a successful voyage across the Atlantic, Jolliet spent the winter in France, where he was given the title of royal pilot. On his return, he began to teach in the Jesuit college in Quebec. The same year, he was granted a small seigneury near Lauzon on the Etchemins River. Though he never had time to develop the land, this is the one of his three seigneuries to bear his name.

The last three years of his life are shrouded in mystery. However, he did sign the parish registry in Quebec on May 4, 1700. On October 18 of the same year, Governor Callière makes reference to Jolliet's death in a letter to France. How he died or where he was buried is still unknown.

In his 50 years, Jolliet travelled from Quebec to Louisiana to Hudson Bay, to Labrador. A brave and modest man, he made his epic journey to the Mississippi without fuss or fanfare. Beyond all doubt, he is one of the greatest and most illustrious names in the history of New France.

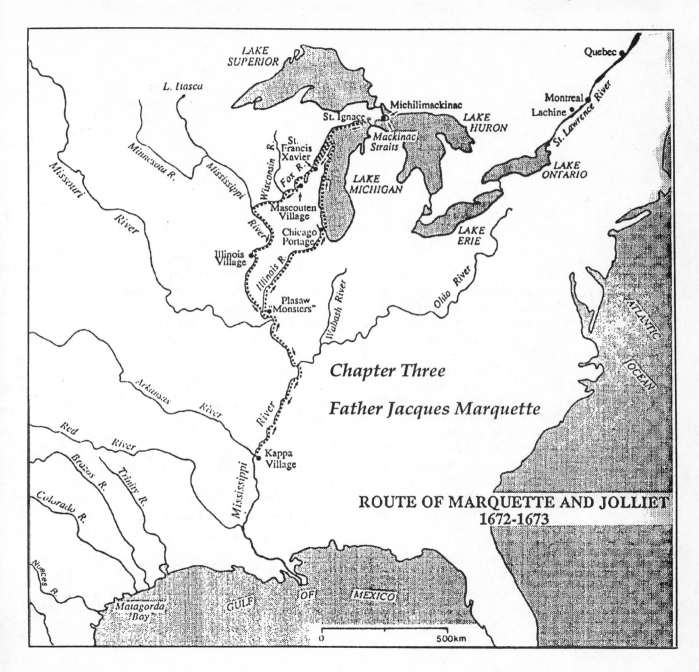

LAKE
SUPERIOR

L. Itasca

Quebec

Montreal
Lachine

St. Lawrence River

Michilimackinac

St. Ignace

Minnesota R.

Mississippi

St.
Francis
Xavier

Wisconsin R.

Fox R.

Mackinac
Straits

LAKE
HURON

LAKE
ONTARIO

Missouri

River

Mascouten
Village

Chicago
Portage

LAKE
MICHIGAN

LAKE
ERIE

Illinois
Village

Illinois R.

Plasaw
"Monsters"

Wabash River

Ohio River

ATLANTIC

River

Chapter Three

OCEAN

Arkansas

River

Father Jacques Marquette

Red

River

Brazos R.

Trinity R.

Mississippi

Kappa
Village

Colorado R.

ROUTE OF MARQUETTE AND JOLLIET
1672-1673

Nueces R.

Matagorda
Bay

GULF   OF   MEXICO

0   500km

Among the first people to venture into the Canadian wilderness were the Jesuit priests. Noble, intelligent and courageous, they risked their lives to spread the gospel among the far-flung Indian villages. The Blackrobes, as the priests were called, won the respect of the native people by sharing their burdens and treating them with respect and kindness. In actual numbers, their converts were few but their influence gained entrance where the fur trader and the explorer might have been excluded. In fact, the Jesuits and the explorers often worked hand in hand. The explorers depended on the influence of the Jesuits and the priests depended on the trade goods and other resources of the explorers.

Two names which are forever linked are those of Louis Jolliet and Father Jacques Marquette, the men who discovered the Mississippi River from the north. Although Jolliet was the official leader of the expedition, the two men worked in harmony. Both were brave, good-hearted adventurers who joyfully risked their lives to discover the great river.

Jacques Marquette came from a noble and respected family in Laon, France. His father, Nicolas, was an important magistrate and his mother, Rose de la Salle, belonged to another distinguished family. As a boy, Jacques went to school with the Jesuits and he entered the order when he was 17. For twelve years he studies and taught in Jesuit seminaries, but his real calling was to be the foreign missions.

Year after year he begged his superiors to allow him to preach in distant lands. When he was 29-years-old, the summons came. A letter arrived from the Jesuits in Canada asking the Father Superior to send new recruits to the missions. The superior chose Father Marquette. With joyful heart, the young priest set sail for the new world and arrived in Quebec on September 20, 1666.

Father Jacques Marquette
Reprinted, by permission, State Historical Society of Wisconsin WHi(X3)9142.

Peace had been proclaimed in the colony that same year. After years of warfare, the French and the Iroquois had finally come to terms. Nevertheless, the cause of the missions looked anything but hopeful. The Huron nation had been scattered by the Iroquois and the once flourishing Jesuit missions destroyed.

A few venturesome priests were pushing their way farther into the interior in an effort to convert the nomadic western tribes. With their altars strapped to their backs, the priests followed their flock from place to place, building and abandoning birch chapels on the way. A few small missions, like those at Sault Ste. Marie and Chequamegon Bay on Lake Superior, had to serve many scattered outposts.

On his arrival in Canada, Father Marquette was sent to the trading post at Trois-Rivières, about 70 miles from Quebec. At the post, he helped Father Dreuillettes in his priestly duties and learned the Montagnais language. Marquette had a knack for languages and Dreuillettes was a good teacher. By 1668, the new missionary knew the native dialects well enough to be sent to the western mission at Sault Ste. Marie. With two donnés and a young Canadian boy, Marquette prepared for his long journey. For greater protection, their canoe joined up with a group of fur traders familiar with the route. Rowing against the current, the little fleet mounted the St. Lawrence to Montreal, then north through strong currents and across many portages on the Ottawa. There were many delays on the way to allow the traders to barter with the native people. At the entrance to Georgian Bay, they manoeuvered their boats past the many beautiful islands nestled in the water until they reached the northern shores of Lake Huron. Skirting the coast past Michilimackinac, they paddled along St. Mary's River to Sault Ste. Marie.

Sault Ste. Marie was an important trading centre. A wild and beautiful place, the settlement was situated at the foot of a raging current of water from Lake Superior. The river abounded in fish. Standing in their canoes, grasping rods with nets like pockets, the native people scooped up the fish, sometimes overturning their boats in the process. When darkness fell, the men often put flares on their canoes and hauled in their catch. There were about 2 000 Algonkians and a few French traders living in the vicinity. Behind a twelve feet high wooden pallisade, the Jesuits had their chapel and mission house. After 10 weeks of travel Father Marquette could begin to teach the native people about Christianity.

It was an uphill struggle. The native people listened politely to his preaching, but they preferred their own religion. After the first glow of optimism dimmed, Marquette had to admit that his only converts were the dying. He pinned his hopes on the children. In their own language, he told them religious stories and presented them with little pictures. He also cultivated a garden and taught the native women how to grow vegetables. Life was comfortable. Father Marquette had a cosy little chapel, a solid roof over his head, and lots of fish and game, and vegetables to eat.

One year later, he was sent three hundred miles farther afield to assume Father Allouez's duties at the new mission on Chequamegon Bay which served the nearby Huron and Ottawa villages. The former priest, Father Allouez, was on his way to Green Bay to found a new mission and Marquette was to take over St. Esprit at Chequamegon.

Marquette set out for his new mission in the ice and snow of an early winter. The Hurons, old allies of the French, welcomed him to their villages but the Ottawas were surly. Spurred on by their medicine men, they openly jeered at the Blackrobe's religion. Only the old and the sick took heed of his words. The wise priest did his best to fit in the new religion with the old ways: "I keep a little of their customs, and take away what is bad." In summer he trekked with them to their fishing grounds and in winter he shared the hardships of the hunt.

He heard about the Mississippi River and about the fertile Illinois plains from Illinois hunters who somtimes visited the mission. Sioux warriors told him similar stories about a river which was three miles wide and about tribes who traded with other white men. The Sioux even promised the priest a safe passage over their land to the far-off tribes. In return, he sent them some of his precious religious pictures. Marquette's heart was filled with excitement; he longed to go to the Mississippi and plant the cross among the far-off tribes.

However, his hopes were rudely dashed. On a hunting trip, the Ottawa made the mistake of attacking the Sioux. The powerful Sioux would not tolerate this breach. Before taking to the warpath, they returned Father Marquette's gifts and ordered the Ottawas and the Hurons to be gone or face the consequences. In frantic haste, the terrified natives gathered their few possessions and left. The Ottawas went to their old home on Manitoulin Island and the Hurons, accompanied by Father Marquette, returned to Michilimackinac. In the summer of 1671, Marquette built a little log chapel on the north shore of the Mackinac Straits and set up the mission of St. Ignace.

The abject Hurons built a pallisaded village nearby. Father Marquette went around from hut to hut, teaching a few prayers to the children and tending to the sick. Since he had no bell to call the people to Mass, he summoned the few faithful himself: "I gladly attended their great pumpkin feast, and bade them be grateful to God for their plentiful harvests." He heard more tales about the great river on visits to far-off camps on the mainland and on the nearby islands.

On December 8, 1672, Louis Jolliet arrived at Michilimackinac with letters from Father Dablon and Governor Frontenac. Marquette's dream had at last come true — he was to accompany Jolliet on a journey to the Mississippi. The priest was now 33-years-old. A kind and gentle man, he knew how to get along with the native people and he spoke seven of their dialects. During the winter while the snow piled up around St. Ignace, the two young men collected every scrap of information they could find about the route and made themselves a rude map.

On the morning of May 17, 1673, the two canoes carrying Marquette, Jolliet and five companions set off from St. Ignace. Behind them on the shore stood Marquette's replacement, Father Pierson and a long line of faithful Hurons. The water gleamed and sparkled in the bright May sunshine as the canoes left the broad harbor and vanished beyond the horizon. The voyageurs, in their tough buckskin suits, plied their oars and Father Marquette, in his long black robes, sat down beside them after placing the expedition under the care of the Virgin Mary.

They coasted along the shores of Lake Michigan, stopping to visit the Menominee Indians near present-day Green Bay. They paused briefly at the St. Francis Mission where Marquette's old friend Father Allouez made them welcome and gave them fresh food supplies. At every native village, Father Marquette told the people about God and handed out a few religious pictures. In his journal, he wrote about the wonderful birds and fish and wild animals on the route. He was astounded by the sight of the buffalo.

> The animal's head is huge, the horns a foot and a half apart, black in color and much longer than those of French cattle. . . . The head, neck, and part of the shoulders are half hidden by a thick and hideous mane which falls over the eyes and must interfere with sight. . . . If an Indian fires at one with either bow or gun he instantly flings himself face downward in the thick grass. Otherwise the wounded animal would charge at him furiously. . . ."

Buffalo
Reprinted, by permission, the Glenbow
Archives, NA-1041-15.

On June 17, "with inexpressible joy," Marquette saw the Mississippi River. At a point near the present boundary of Arkansas and Louisiana the party turned their canoes for home. They had explored the Mississippi for 1 000 miles and they knew that it flowed into the Gulf of Mexico. It would be foolhardy for the little band to penetrate into Spanish territory.

On the way back, Father Marquette wrote very little in his journal. His seven years in the western missions and the long voyage to the Mississippi were beginning to take their toll. Seven miles below the present city of Ottawa, the canoes came to an Illinois settlement of 74 cabins, where the tired travellers rested for three days. Best of all

the tribes, Father Marquette loved "the gentle Illinois." In their courteous fashion, they listened to the words of their Blackrobe visitor and invited him to return and set up a mission in their territory.

By the end of October, the party was back in Green Bay at the mission of St. Francis Xavier. Here Father Marquette remained to rest and regain his health. By spring he was feeling better and eager to return to his Illinois friends to found a mission. No sooner had he received permission from his superiors than he was off again.

With two companions, Pierre and Jacques, Father Marquette set out from Green Bay on October 25. It was late in the season for such a journey, especially for a man in failing health. At the western shore of Lake Michigan, they were joined by several native canoes. As they travelled along the western shores of the lake, the cold became more intense and lashing gales forced the men to take shelter. By the end of November, heavy snow lay on the ground, game was scarce and Father Marquette was becoming weaker and weaker. Near the present-day city of Chicago, he knew he could go no farther. A halt was called and the two boatmen built a wooden shelter.

Marquette remained in the hut from December to March, while his two companions tended to his needs. Now and then, friendly natives came to visit him bringing gifts of corn, pumpkins and dried meat. In return for a little tobacco, he received three oxskins to cover himself and his two companions in the cold winter nights. Two French traders, who were wintering about 150 miles away, also came to visit bringing with them some meal and some dried blackberries. In those days, any kind of fruit was a rare delicacy in winter.

By the middle of March, Father Marquette began to feel better and the three travellers were off again. Trudging through the muddy portage they made their way to the Des Plaines River, swollen by the spring floods, until they reached the junction of the Illinois River. Shortly after, they reached the Illinois village (near the present Utica) where Father Marquette was received "like an angel from Heaven."

The priest set to work with a will. Weak as he was, he visited the wigwams, talked to the chiefs and when he thought they were ready he called them to a great council. Displaying four large pictures of the Virgin Mary which he had managed to preserve from the winter elements he told the large audience about the white man's religion. Then he parted with his last gifts. The natives listened politely to the sermon and the chiefs begged him to remain in the village.

Father Marquette longed to remain with his favorite flock, but he knew his end was near. Before his death, he wanted to see a priest and confess his sins. Bidding farewell to the Illinois, he promised to send them a Blackrobe in his stead. In a few days, he left for Michilimackinac with all the supplies the canoes could carry and a bodyguard of Illinois warriors to escort him to Lake Michigan.

Launching their canoe on the lake the two boatmen paddled along the eastern shore while Father Marquette lay down on his mat. Barely able to say his prayers, Father Marquette became frailer with each passing day. Close to a green hillock by the shore he asked the men to help him disembark. On a green sward by the river that now bears his name, they laid him down by a freshly lighted fire. Marquette then thanked them for their kindness and heard their confessions. In a few hours he was dead. His companions buried him in the quiet wilderness, his beads and his crucifix on his breast. The boatmen made their way to Michilimackinac, to the little mission at St. Ignace, bringing the priest's journal and his few worldly possession with them.

For two years, the grave, topped by a small wooden cross, remained undisturbed. A couple of years later, a group of native people hunting by the shores of Lake Michigan came to the spot where their former missionary was buried. With great reverence they disinterred the body, washed the bones according to their custom and carried them with them in a wooden box to St. Ignace. After a solemn requiem Mass in the mission chapel, the remains were buried beneath the chapel floor.

For a time, Michilimackinac bustled with the activity of trappers, traders and native people. Twelve shops bulging with shirts, mirrors, knives, tobacco and other objects of the white man's culture lined the shore. In the centre of the town, stood the pallisaded chapel and mission house that ministered to the nearby Hurons. Close to the shore stood another Jesuit mission house for the Ottawa tribes. For 25 years, the memory of Father Marquette was kept fresh among French and native people alike.

In 1701, Antoine de La Mothe Cadillac received permission to build a fort at Detroit. Cadillac attracted many of the native people from Michilimackinac to this fort. For a time, the Jesuits remained in their old home ministering to their remaining flock, but in 1706 they gave up. Taking their holy vessels and vestments with them, they burned the chapel to prevent it from being desecrated. About 200 years after Marquette's death, fragments of bones believed to be those of the dead priest were found under the site of the burnt log chapel. The bones are now preserved in the Marquette University in Milwaukee.

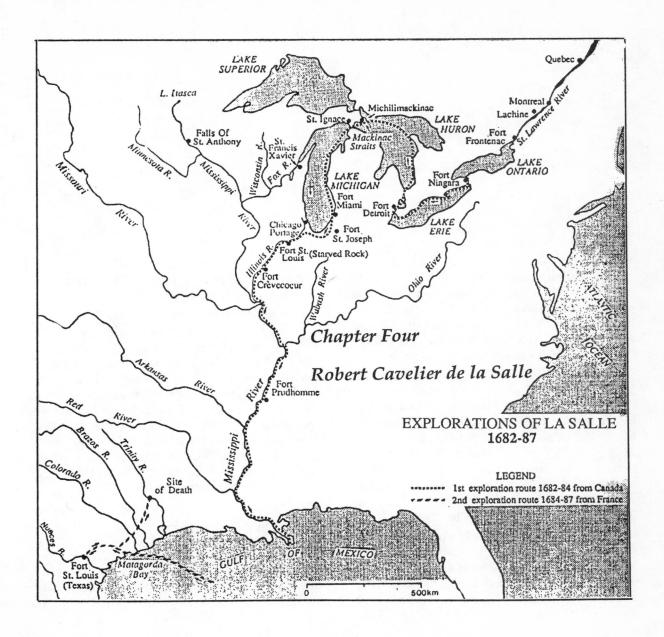

LAKE SUPERIOR

L. Itasca

Quebec

Montreal
Lachine

Michilimackinac

St. Ignace

LAKE HURON

Fort Frontenac

St. Lawrence River

Falls Of St. Anthony

St. Francis Xavier

Mackinac Straits

LAKE ONTARIO

Minnesota R.

Wisconsin R.

Fox R.

Fort Niagara

Mississippi River

LAKE MICHIGAN

Fort Miami

Fort Detroit

Missouri River

Chicago Portage

Fort St. Joseph

LAKE ERIE

Illinois R.

Fort St. Louis (Starved Rock)

Fort Crèvecœur

Wabush River

Ohio River

ATLANTIC OCEAN

Arkansas River

Mississippi River

Chapter Four

Robert Cavelier de la Salle

Fort Prudhomme

Red River

River

EXPLORATIONS OF LA SALLE
1682-87

Brazos R.

Trinity R.

Colorado R.

Mississippi

Site of Death

LEGEND

Nueces R.

•••••••• 1st exploration route 1682-84 from Canada
– – – – – 2nd exploration route 1684-87 from France

Fort St. Louis (Texas)

Matagorda Bay

GULF OF MEXICO

0   500km

In Rouen, France, there lived a proud and wealthy family named Cavelier. For generations, many members of the family had served their country well, but the one who brought glory to their name was Robert Cavelier, better known to us as La Salle.

La Salle was born on November 21, 1643, the second son of a well-to-do merchant. As a boy, he went to school at the Jesuit college in Rouen and he later entered the order. In some ways, he had the makings of a good priest. He was a serious young man and an excellent student, especially in science and mathematics. What stood in his way was his independent character; it was in his nature to command, not to obey.

When La Salle was 24-years-old he left the order. Under church law, he had been forced to renounce all claims to his father's estate when he entered the Jesuits. On the death of his father, the estate was divided among the other heirs, leaving young Robert penniless except for a small allowance given to him by his family. With this money in his pocket, he set out for Canada.

His brother Jean was a Sulpician priest in Montreal. The Sulpicians, who owned all the land in the Montreal settlement, granted La Salle a large tract of land at Lachine. Both parties benefitted from this arrangement. The priests benefitted because of the resulting buffer against Iroquois attacks and the land would be cleared. La Salle benefitted because he received the property for next to nothing in a good fur-trading area. With any luck he could become a rich man.

Like a good seigneur, La Salle encouraged families to settle on his new estate. He built a high pallisade to protect his new residents against Iroquois attacks. Inside the pallisade were homes and small plots of land, and outside were larger holdings. The life of a seigneur soon began to pall, for La Salle craved glory and adventure, not security or riches.

Robert Cavelier, Sieur de la Salle
Courtesy of Harvard College Library

He heard of a great river which the Senecas called the Ohio or "beautiful river." According to their stories, the river flowed over a vast stretch of country and emptied into the western sea. His imagination stirred, he dreamt of discovering the fabled passage to China. For La Salle, to dream was to act. He would follow the great river and see where it led.

First he had to get permission from Intendant Talon and Governor de Courcelle. Talon liked the plan but he could offer no money to carry it through; if La Salle wanted to go exploring, he would have to bear the cost himself. Nothing daunted, he went to Montreal and sold his land back to the Sulpicians at a good profit. The Sulpicians were anxious to spread the gospel into the far west, and one of their number was Father Dollier de Casson who was already in Montreal preparing for a voyage into the unknown wilderness. At Talon's suggestion, La Salle and the Sulpicians joined forces.

On July 6, 1699 the party set out for Seneca country. As ill-luck would have it, a Seneca chief had just been murdered by three drunken soldiers in Montreal. Although the soldiers had been executed for the deed, the Senecas harbored a grudge. Nevertheless, the nine canoes carrying twenty-two men sailed up the St. Lawrence River toward Lake Ontario. It was a harsh journey. After paddling and portaging all day, they laid themselves to rest at night on the bare earth. According to one of the priests, they had "to peel bark from the trees and make a shed by laying it on a frame of sticks" to shelter themselves from the rain. Their food, consisting of Indian corn mixed with meat and fish, made many of them sick. Early in August, the party reached the shores of Lake Ontario.

Crossing the lake, they travelled south to Seneca country, where they met some of the natives and were invited to the village. After a solemn welcome by the elders, a large feast was prepared in their honor and the children brought them berries and pumpkins.

La Salle, however, did not understand the language as well as he thought, and thus he was unable to make himself understood. Compounding this difficulty, the Dutchman who had accompanied the priests as an interpreter, could speak Iroquois but almost no French. The Seneca chief, who happened to be a relative of the man murdered in Montreal, became more and more hostile. After a month of useless parleys, the Seneca council flatly refused to give La Salle a guide to the river.

The impasse was broken by the arrival of a lone Iroquois on his way to his home near present-day Hamilton, Ontario. The man promised to guide them to his village and from there they would find a good route to the Ohio. On their arrival, they met Louis Jolliet's brother, Adrien, on his way home from Lake Superior. The meeting was a momentous one. Jolliet's stories about the Potawatomis in the northwest, who had still not heard the word of God, spurred the Sulpicians to set out in that direction.

La Salle had a different idea. A few days earlier he had been ill with fever and according to himself, he would have to return to Montreal to recover. No doubt he was glad to get rid of the priests because he disliked sharing the command with others.

What he did or where he went after the priests left is uncertain; however, one thing is clear, he did not return to Montreal. For three years he remained in the wilderness, his whereabouts a mystery. In the summer of 1670, he was seen hunting on the Ottawa River. Some people say he discovered the Ohio River, while others even say he discovered the Mississippi before Jolliet, though that seems unlikely. Wherever he was, his years in the wilderness taught him

how to survive hardships, how to find his way from river to lake to stream, and how to get along with the native people. It was probably during this time that he planned his grand design – the establishment of an inland trading empire linked by great waterways and stretching from the Great Lakes to the mouth of the Mississippi.

When La Salle reappeared in Quebec, Frontenac was the new governor. A bold and ambitious man, Frontenac wanted to keep the Iroquois in check and extend the frontiers of New France. His first plan was to build a fort on the north shore of Lake Ontario at Cataracoui (near present-day Kingston). La Salle was chosen to go down to Iroquois country and persuade the chiefs to come to Cataracoui to meet the Governor.

La Salle did his job well. The meeting was a great success, peace was proclaimed and a French fort, to be named Fort Frontenac, was built on the site. Well pleased with everything, Frontenac returned to Quebec and La Salle remained in Fort Frontenac to oversee the building.

The fur traders in Montreal were up in arms. The new fort could spell the ruin of their own fur trade because the western natives would likely stop at the fort to do their trading instead of making the long journey to Montreal. Before long the whole colony was in an uproar. Throughout the bitter dispute, La Salle threw his full support behind Governor Frontenac.

La Salle's loyalty to Frontenac stood him in good stead. In the autumn of 1674, he crossed over to France, carrying with him glowing references from the Governor. His visit was a complete success. He was granted Fort Frontenac on condition that he raise a stone fort, and he also received a title of nobility. In return, he promised to bring out settlers, to build a church and to support a few Recollet priests.

In Fort Frontenac, La Salle was master of an enormous expanse of land. With the help of loans from his family, he built a stone fort and paid a garrison to protect it. A mill and a bakery were constructed for the convenience of the settlers, and Recollet priests were installed in their own little church. With his large boats, he did a brisk fur-trading business with the native people, thus diverting profits from the French in Montreal and the English in Albany. He had the solitude that he liked and complete control over his domain. All this was only a stepping-stone toward larger goals. In a few years, he was back in France with his plan to establish other trading posts in unexplored land. He was well received and he was given permission to set up a line of forts as far as the Gulf of Mexico, the project to be completed in five years. He received the monopoly over buffalo hides, but he was forbidden to do any fur-trading with the western natives.

His great work was about to begin. What he needed now was money, a lot of money. Men, ships, supplies, ammunition, all had to be obtained and paid for out of his own pocket. With visions of the vast profits to be made on the venture, his own family and other speculators lent him the necessary funds. While he was in France he also met Henry de Tonty, who became his able and faithful lieutenant.

To begin his trading empire, he planned to construct a fort at Niagara. A ship would be built there which could transport goods and materials across the lakes. While La Salle was making final preparations for the expedition, he sent a group of workmen ahead to Niagara to commence work on the fort. The men arrived at their destination in November. It was bitterly cold and the men had to pour boiling water on the frozen ground before they could set down the foundations. The Senecas were unfriendly because they feared that the new fort would interrupt their fur trade.

With the arrival of La Salle, Tonty, and the rest of the force, the men took heart. Then, the first of many disasters struck. The pilot of the supply ship ran the vessel aground and everything aboard was lost. It was a crushing blow to La Salle who was already deeply in debt. Nevertheless, supplies had to be obtained, and La Salle and two men set out on foot for Fort Frontenac.

It was February, the coldest month in the year, and Fort Frontenac was 250 miles away. Dogs pulled the baggage and sleds, while the men battled the wind and snow. They had hardly anything to eat except Indian corn, and even that ran out toward the end. Rumors of the disaster had preceded La Salle to Fort Frontenac and some of his creditors had seized his property. His enemies were saying that he was a madman, embarking on a reckless journey from which he would never return. With great difficulty he managed to put off his creditors and returned again to Niagara.

During La Salle's absence, the workmen under Tonty's direction had completed work on the boat. Christened the *Griffin* it was a 45 ton sailing vessel armed with five cannons and the mythical beast after which it was named carved on its hull. After a blessing by Father Hennepin and a cannon roll, the boat was launched into the waters of Lake Erie. For a few days, the ship glided peacefully over the smooth waters; however, at the entrance to Lake Huron, the wind strengthened into a gale and the ship tossed wildly on the boiling current. Even La Salle feared the worst. Falling on his knees with the others, he prayed to God to save them all. The storm abated and the ship arrived safely in the peaceful harbor of Michilimackinac.

Cannons boomed out and the inhabitants rushed to the shore to view the great ship, the first sailing vessel ever seen on the lakes. In a scarlet cloak trimmed with gold, La Salle disembarked and marched with his men to the Jesuit church for a Mass of thanksgiving. Afterwards, the Huron and Ottawa chiefs made solemn speeches of welcome.

In reality, La Salle was anything but welcome at Michilimackinac. His great boat would spell ruin for the local fur traders who had only their small canoes to transport their furs. It was true that he had been forbidden to trade in the area, but as a friend of Governor Frontenac, the ban might be lifted. Some of his men had already been trading in the vicinity and whether they were egged on by his enemies or not, had either absconded with his goods or were wasting his money in drinking and carousing. La Salle arrested the deserters that had remained in Michilimackinac and sent Tonty to Sault Ste. Marie to round up the rest.

La Salle then set off in the *Griffin* for Green Bay. The situation was better at the bay. His advance party had worked diligently to collect a large stock of furs, which he sorely needed to pay off his creditors. At this stage, he made a decision which was to cost him dearly. He dispatched the *Griffin* to Niagara with orders to the crew to return to the head of Lake Michigan to meet him. The ill-starred boat with its valuable cargo set out from Green Bay on September 18 and was never heard from again. Meanwhile, La Salle and the fourteen men who still remained turned south in four canoes laden with tools, arms and even a blacksmith's forge, toward the mouth of the St. Joseph River (which La Salle named the Miami). Fierce storms battered the canoes, almost crushing them against the rocks. Several times the men had to beach their heavy craft at the peril of their lives. One priest, Father Gabriel Membré, a cheerful man of 64, fell sick, but he never complained, even when he was plunged into the icy water. Hunger plagued the party as well. Reduced to a diet of pumpkin and dried corn, their spirits rose when they saw the smoke of a native village. However, the natives fled to the forest at the sight of them. The travellers found a stock of corn in the village and left trade goods in exchange. The next day, the native people returned to the village and gave the party some very welcome venison.

Worn out with hardship and hunger, the expedition reached the mouth of the St. Joseph in early November. While awaiting Tonty's arrival, La Salle erected a fort. For twenty days the men worked, as the weather became colder and food supplies dwindled. Worn out, tired and afraid of starvation, they urged La Salle to move on to the great village of the Illinois. La Salle was adamant; he would wait until Tonty arrived.

Tonty arrived in early December, but he had no word of the *Griffin*. More than enough time had passed for the ship to reach Niagara, unload the cargo and return. Day after day La Salle's eyes scanned the horizon in vain. When he could wait no longer, he sent two men to Michilimackinac to find out about the ship. Then he and his 33 men sailed up the St. Joseph River to a place where there was a curve in the river (near present-day South Bend, Indiana). A portage from there would take them to the Illinois River. The day they reached the portage, La Salle's Mohegan guide, Nika, was scouting for game in the woods and without his guidance the men overshot the landing.

La Salle went ashore to search for the crossing. Trudging through the dense forest in swirling snow he lost his way in the gathering darkness. About two o'clock in the morning, he saw firelight gleaming in the darkness. The fire had been lit by a native who had fled at the sound of La Salle's approach. Cold and tired, the explorer lay down on a heap of dry grass by the warm fire and slept until daylight. In the morning, he set out again and rejoined his companions in safety.

Dragging the heavy boats across the 5 mile portage was heavy work, especially in the middle of winter. Day by day, the men became more sullen and disheartened with the expedition. One of them would have shot La Salle in the back, if someone hadn't knocked the gun out of the man's hand. However, there were two people who could always be depended on, Tonty and the Mohegan guide Nika.

The lights of the Illinois village (near the present Peoria) were a welcome sight. At first, La Salle was well received. As a token of their esteem, the Illinois rubbed the men with grease and oil and they fed them with their own fingers. The peace pipe was passed around and La Salle told them about his proposed journey and his intention to protect them against their old enemies, the Iroquois.

The next day it was a different story. A visitor had reached the Illinois during the night with a story he had heard from some of La Salle's enemies. According to him, La Salle was a spy, planning to stir up the Iroquois against the Illinois. Luckily for the explorer, he got wind of the story and made his way to the chiefs to deny it. Although they accepted his explanation for the time being, they were far from satisfied. Trying to keep him from proceeding, they told him fearful tales about savage tribes and man-eating alligators. The following night six of his men took to their heels in fright, taking some of the supplies with them.

This was a great blow to La Salle. He could ill afford to lose the six men, especially since two of them happened to be good carpenters. Knowing that the Illinois would be suspicious about the desertions, he decided to move his camp a few miles from the village. On a hill overlooking the river he erected a pallisaded fort aptly called Fort Crèvecoeur (or Fort Heartbreak).

Poor La Salle must indeed have been heartbroken, as one disaster followed another. The *Griffin* was almost certainly lost, his men were deserting, his creditors were closing in on him, and his enemies were turning the native people against him. Despite the odds, he never swerved from his resolution. Another ship would have to be built to operate on the Mississippi. With his own hands, he designed and laid the foundation of the new boat. After six weeks of hard labor, when the boat was half-completed, he sent two experienced voyageurs, Michel Accou and Picard du Guay, with Father Louis Hennepin to explore the upper reaches of the Mississippi. La Salle knew he would have to return to Fort Frontenac for rigging, sails and other supplies to complete the vessel. Leaving Tonty in charge at Fort Crèvecoeur, he set off on the 1 000 mile journey bringing four Frenchmen and the Mohegan guide, Nika, with him.

Through the thaws of the approaching spring, the six men set off on the gruelling journey. As the two canoes paddled farther north, the waters were often frozen over and the men had to shoulder their craft through the sodden marshes along the shore. When they could, they broke the ice with their hatchets and manoeuvred the canoes through lumps of floating ice. Weary and often without enough to eat, they slept on the cold earth. Near the present-day town of Jolliet, Illinois, the thick ice made the water impassable. So, they hid their canoes and continued on foot.

The men had to shoulder their canoes over portages. Reprint, by permission, Glenbow Archives NA-4474-23.

Reaching a river that was already thawed, they made a raft of hardwood timber to carry them to the other side. In La Salle's own words: "The rain which lasted all day and the raft we were obliged to make to pass over the water stopped us until noon of the twenty-fifth, when we continued our march through the woods which were so intertwined with thorns and brambles that in two days our clothes were all torn and our faces so covered in blood that we hardly knew each other."

At the shores of Lake Michigan, La Salle had news from two men who had been sent forward to find word of the *Griffin*. They had heard or seen nothing of the boat. There was no room for any further hope – the boat had to be given up for lost. La Salle and his men forged ahead. After a journey of two and a half days, the woods opened into prairies and the game became more plentiful. Unfortunately, the rigors of the journey began to tell. One by one the men became sick and a canoe had to be built to transport them. Finally, two of them had to be sent to Michilimackinac to recover and the rest proceeded in another canoe to Fort Niagara.

The news at Niagara was not hopeful. A ship from France bearing twenty men and valuable goods had sunk in the St. Lawrence and La Salle's creditors had seized his property at Fort Frontenac. Still undaunted, he sent men and supplies to Tonty at Crèvecoeur and hurried on to Fort Frontenac and Montreal. At Montreal he learned that a cargo of furs had been wrecked on the Lachine rapids.

After dealing with his creditors in Montreal, La Salle set out again for Fort Crèvecouer. Upon reaching Fort Frontenac two wandering trappers brought word of further treachery. Tonty's men had mutineed and destroyed the new fort. Not content with this destruction, the deserters had gone on to Michilimackinac and seized his furs and later plundered the fort at Niagara. Before going to Tonty's help, La Salle had to chase the thieves and recover what he could from them.

In spite of all these calamities, La Salle never faltered. At least, he could depend on the faithful Tonty. Even yet, it might be possible to finish the ship and sail down the river. Gathering another twenty-five men, the explorer set out on the long trail to the Illinois country. At the great Illinois village near Fort Crèvecoeur, a scene of horror met their eyes. The village was a wasteland, huts in ruins, corn fields burned and storehouses ransacked. Wolves prowled over the land, and corpses littered the once bustling village. La Salle and his men searched the grim wreckage for a sign of Tonty's body, but no body was found.

Further down the river, they came to Fort Crèvecoeur, deserted and in ruins. Still hoping to come upon Tonty, La Salle pushed on to the mouth of the Illinois River. Before him stretched the broad Mississippi, the fatal river of his dreams, but he took no joy in the sight. Leaving a letter for Tonty in an overhanging branch in case he should come that way, La Salle paddled back. On his way up the river, his spirits rose when he saw a wooden hut and a piece of wood marked by the teeth of a saw. He knew the native people had no such tool. Perhaps Tonty had passed that way and was still safe and sound somewhere.

He spent the winter at Fort Miami on the St. Joseph River where there was a fort to shelter the party from the cold. La Salle was not idle. With the help of his Mohegan hunter, he travelled to the neighboring tribes, making peace treaties and offering protection from the Iroquois. Always more successful in his dealings with the native people than he was with his fellow countrymen, he managed to attract many tribes to his side.

In May he was back in Michilimackinac, where he was reunited with Tonty and Father Membré. In spite of all his misfortunes, La Salle was calm and undefeated. As Father Membré says, "Anyone else would abandon the enterprise, but Monsieur de la Salle has no equal for constancy of purpose."

For the last time, he set out for Montreal, taking Tonty with him. He would make another effort to appease his creditors and get what he needed to continue the exploration. He had a good friend in Governor Frontenac. With the governor's help he managed to get his business affairs in order and to get extra loans from his relatives. After making his will in favor of a cousin who advanced him some money, he set out once more.

This time he had thirty Frenchmen and several native people and their wives with him. The natives would be valuable helpers. They were skilled hunters who could be relied upon to provide game for the party, and some of them could speak the languages of the southern tribes. The women could cook and help with the camp chores. Following the route through Lake Ontario, Lake Huron and Lake Michigan, the heavily laden canoes reached Fort Miami on December 21, 1681.

After a brief rest at the fort, the party set off for Fort Crèvecoeur. It was the dead of winter and the river was covered by a thick crust of ice. Turning the canoes into sleds, the party slid down the frozen Illinois River or walked by its banks for 120 miles until they reached the fort.

From there the river was clear. Launching their canoes, the motley group of natives, soldiers, voyageurs, women and one priest paddled along until they entered the broad waters of the Mississippi.

The worst of the journey was over. They paddled peacefully along, past the muddy junction of the Missouri and the mouth of the Ohio, stopping occasionally to hunt for game. Near present-day Memphis, Tennessee, they camped for the night and some of the men hunted for game. One of the hunters, a locksmith named Pierre Prudhomme lost his way and was found six days later. To cheer the poor man, who had been wandering through swamp and forest, La Salle gave the new fort the name Fort Prudhomme and left the locksmith and a few men in charge of it.

The party continued down the widening river. It was now March. Day by day the trees were shooting out new buds, and the weather was warm and balmy while morning mists swirled over the waters. The water teemed with catfish and the shore yielded an abundance of deer, buffalo, woodcock and wild turkeys.

One foggy evening the silence was broken by the sounds of war cries and battle drums from the right shore. Swiftly steering for the left bank, La Salle and his men built a rough fort. When the fog cleared, some of the natives cautiously approached the fort in a large wooden canoe made from a hollow tree. The French had nothing to fear. The friendly visitors belonged to the powerful and hospitable Arkansas tribe, living in the town of Kappa on the Arkansas River.

Crossing over the river, the French found themselves in a prosperous village. The chief came to welcome them and escorted them to a special house where they feasted royally for three days. Many dances were preformed in their honor and Father Membré preached a sermon in French to which the Arkansas listened politely, though they didn't understand a word he was saying. Before their departure, La Salle and his men marched to an open square where they erected the arms of King Louis. Unknown to their hospitable hosts, the land was claimed for the King of France!

With extra supplies of food, and two guides supplied by the Arkansas, the party continued to another tribe of the Arkansas nation called the Taensas. The village was a beautiful sight. Several large adobe houses were built around a square bordered by vines and many varieties of fruit and nut trees. The largest house belonged to the chief who sat in regal splendor surrounded by three wives and 60 warriors in white robes made from mulberry bark. Close to the royal residence was a temple with an altar before which burned a perpetual fire tended by two old priests.

La Salle did not see all the fine sights, for he was ill and had to remain on the opposite bank of the river. To honor him, the chief crossed the river to visit him. Preceded by two men carrying fans of white feathers and by two others carrying highly polished disks, he presented himself to La Salle and the two men exchanged courtesies.

Although unwilling to leave their friendly hosts, the French set off again the next day. As they descended the river, they saw a lone canoe with several natives on board. No doubt fearing an enemy attack, La Salle sent Tonty forward to give chase. Just as Tonty was almost abreast of the boat, La Salle spotted numerous native people on the shore with bows and arrows ready to defend their friends. Calling out frantically to Tonty, La Salle told him to proceed to the shore with the peace pipe. At the sight of the pipe, the men laid down the weapons and again the French were presented with a feast and given shelter for the night. Only once on the rest of the journey were they greeted with a shower of arrows. On that occasion, La Salle prudently ordered his men to move to safety on the other side of the river.

At last they came to a point where the Mississippi divided into three channels. La Salle took the western channel, Tonty took the middle and another man followed the eastern stream. In a few miles, the fresh water turned to brine and the vast stretches of the Gulf of Mexico sparkled before them. On April 7, 1682, on a mound above the mouth of the river, La Salle donned his scarlet and gold cloak and raised the arms of King Louis. For the first time, a European had travelled from the St. Lawrence to the mouth of the Mississippi.

The assembled group chanted prayers of thanksgiving and La Salle took possession of the vast country which he called Louisiana, in the name of the French King. To shouts of "Vive le Roi," the men fired their muskets and a metal plaque engraved with the King's name and the date was fixed on a pillar in the soil. The King of France was now lord over a vast territory stretching from the mouth of the Ohio to the Gulf of Mexico.

After so many trials, La Salle had achieved one of his greatest goals. He had reached the mouth of "the fatal river." However, there was no time to tarry and explore farther. Much remained to be done before the great trading empire was established. Three days later, the party set off on the long homeward journey. For six days, they lived on alligator flesh and a few potatoes. On they went, stopping at native villages, some friendly, some unfriendly, until they came to Fort Prudhomme.

The hardships he had endured for the last several years were beginning to tell on La Salle. At Fort Prudhomme he was stricken with an illness which laid him low for 40 days. When he was well enough to travel, he slowly made his way to Michilimackinac to rejoin Tonty, who had been sent ahead.

La Salle's illness prevented him from proceeding immediately to Montreal. In a letter to a friend in France he said he had hardly enough strength to take up his pen and he was afraid that the hungers and hardships of the long journey would kill him. Meanwhile, he sent Tonty back to the Illinois country to prepare the way for the new trading colony to be built there. In late December, La Salle was well enough to join Tonty. A site for the new fort was chosen at a place called Starved Rock. The flat rock about an acre across arose to a height of 125 feet above the Illinois River and was accessible from one side. A fort surrounded by pallisades was built and named Fort St. Louis.

During the winter, he met with several tribes and encouraged them to settle near the fort. By his own account, 20 000 people were gathered together in the vast Illinois prairies, all under his protection. A score of French settlers had also arrived and were given parcels of land nearby.

Buried in the Illinois wilderness, La Salle was unaware of what was happening in Quebec. A new governor, an avaricious man named Le Febvre de la Barre had replaced Frontenac. From the beginning, La Barre did all in his power to ruin La Salle. When La Salle asked for soldiers to protect the new colony from an expected Iroquois attack, the governor did nothing. Instead he sent letters to France complaining loudly about the explorer. According to the letters, La Salle was inciting the Iroquois, he was living like a king, and he should be forced to return to Quebec to face his creditors. The governor even went so far as to say that La Salle had invented the whole story of his discovery of the Mississippi.

All these complaints had their effect. Before long, a letter arrived from the court telling La Barre to proceed against the explorer. Thereupon La Barre seized Fort Frontenac and sold all La Salle's goods. Meanwhile, the explorer was stranded in Fort St. Louis expecting an Iroquois attack at any moment, while the unhappy native tribes around the fort were imploring the help he had no means to provide. Luckily, the Iroquois attack did not take place, but La Salle knew that something would have to be done to clear his name and to keep the Illinois colony afloat. In 1683 he sailed to France.

Paris was buzzing with stories of La Salle's exploits. Soon after his arrival, he had an interview with the King and presented a bold new proposal. He would establish a colony 60 miles up the Mississippi River, and from there, an attack could be launched against the Spaniards in northern Mexico. With the help of 200 men from France, the freebooters he could recruit in San Domingo, and his French and native followers in Canada he would be able to drive the Spaniards from North America. The map of the Mississippi which he presented at court made it look as though the river was much nearer to Mexico than it really was.

No one in France was able to dispute his calculations. They knew little about the geography of North America and less about the dangers of such an expedition. That one man, crippled with debts and with only a small force could conquer a vast continent should surely have seemed impossible. Nevertheless, the King and his ministers let themselves be lured by dreams of gold and huge possessions.

Once more the sun was shining on La Salle. The King wrote to La Barre ordering the governor to return all the explorer's property. For his new undertaking, La Salle was to have four ships and the men and supplies he needed. The warship the *Joly* was to be commanded by Taneguy de Beaujeu, an experienced officer, but the overall command belonged to La Salle. The expedition got off to a bad start; some of the soldiers were a poor lot, poorly trained and unable to fire a musket. Of the so-called artisans, a large number were later found to know nothing about their trades. La Salle and Beaujeu detested one another and were unable to agree about anything. La Salle, who had no definite plans for the expeditions, was so secretive about everything that Beaujeu was unaware of their exact destination. On his side, Beaujeu considered La Salle an upstart, without any knowledge of naval matters.

After several weeks of bickering, the ill-fated expedition was ready. There were about 400 people on board – soldiers, tradesmen, priests, and a few families, women and children included. La Salle's brother, Father Jean Cavelier, and his young nephew, Moranget, were also of the party.

On July 24, 1684 the four ships sailed out from La Rochelle harbor. First came the warship the *Joly*, followed by another armed vessel the *Belle*, then the supply and ammunition ship the *Aimable*, and lastly a small craft, the *St. François* also carrying food. They were hardly out of the harbor when the *Joly* broke her bowsprit and had to return to port, where the damage was soon repaired. As they plied their way toward the French West Indies, the heat became intense and the two leaders continued to quarrel about everything, from the filling of water casks to the best place to anchor in the islands.

The heat and lack of water began to take their toll on the men. In those days, when a ship crossed the Tropic of Cancer it was customary for the sailors to be allowed to "baptize" in a tub of water anyone who had not yet crossed the line. Anyone who refused to be "baptized" had to give the sailors a gift of money or liquor. It was all a merry game which brought the sailors some extra revenue, but La Salle refused to permit it – thus making himself very unpopular with the crew.

By the time the ships reached San Domingo, La Salle himself was very unwell. While the sick man tossed feverishly in his bed, in a wretched garret, there was no one to keep control over the men and the expedition began to fall apart. Some of the people deserted; others drank, and caroused and picked up diseases. To add to the general misfortune, Spanish pirates captured the store ship *Aimable*. In late November, the haggard and gloomy La Salle was well enough to travel and the fleet, now reduced to three, set out again. Passing the Cayman Island and hugging the coast of Cuba they continued cautiously into the Gulf of Mexico, from which foreign ships were excluded by Spain.

No one in command knew much about the coastline; it was up to La Salle to identify the mouth of the Mississippi. He knew the latitude of his post, but like others of his day, he knew little about longitude. One inlet in the marshy coastline looked very much like another and before long his ship had sailed more than 300 miles too far west.

La Salle was lost and he knew it.

Tempers were rising and the passengers were becoming more and more disheartened. The three ships were continually being separated from each other in the fogs and storms. At length, he saw a harbor with three large inlets and he took it into his head that the harbor was one of the western arms of the Mississippi. He decided to land. Once ashore they could explore the coast until they found the mouth of the river. In fact the party was at the entrance of Matagorda Bay, Texas about 400 miles from the Mississippi Delta.

It was a broad harbor obstructed by a vast sandbar. Though it was too shallow for the *Joly*, the *Belle* entered without much difficulty. Whether by accident or design, the captain of the *Aimable* made a sailing error and ran the ship aground. La Salle did his best to save the cargo. Only a small quantity of gunpowder and a few barrels of flour and pork were hauled ashore before a storm came on and the huge waves carried most of the meal, vegetables, utensils and ammunition out to sea. Meanwhile, a few local natives managed to steal some blankets and the French retaliated by stealing the native boat. A fight broke out and two of the Frenchmen were killed and two injured.

Beaujeu left for France on March 12, taking several of the disappointed colonists with him. He had lingered on as long as he could but he could no longer remain in the Gulf in case of an attack by the Spaniards. The two men parted on good terms. Beaujeu even offered to go to Martinque to fetch provisions for the sorry band of colonists, but La Salle declined the offer. He thought Martinque wouldn't help; besides he probably didn't want to run up any more debts.

It must have been with a sense of foreboding that the hapless people saw the ship depart. Fearing a native attack, La Salle ordered a fort to be built from the wreckage of the *Aimable*. When the fort was nearly finished he set out with fifty men to search for the Mississippi, leaving a dependable subordinate, Henri Joutel, in charge of the 130 who remained. Many trials took place at the new fort in La Salle's absence. The site was unhealthy and several people died of dysentry and yellow fever. As he was wading through a stream in search of game, one of the men was bitten by a rattlesnake and later died. At night the natives prowled about the camp, but they were put to flight without any loss of life.

Meanwhile, La Salle returned to the camp. In his explorations he had found a better spot for a settlement – on a hill a few miles away on a river called La Vache, or Cow River, now known as Lavacq. One big drawback was the scarcity of timber, and the wood had to be hauled for a few miles to the site so that, as Joutel says, "the ablest men were quite worn out." La Salle's nerves were at the breaking point. Nothing was working out as he had planned "which often made him insult the men when there was little reason." By the time the new Fort St. Louis was finished, thirty more men had died and the sick bay was crowded with the sick and dying.

By the end of October, the ramshackle buildings were built, with a pallisade, and cannons mounted in the four corners. La Salle's next plan was to send his brother and Joutel to Quebec and then to France for help, while he would arrange for a rescue party from Tonty's post on the Illinois. To make clothes for the expedition the men collected sheets, scraps of linen, and canvas from the *Belle*. When they were almost ready to depart, another misfortune befell them. Worn out by fatigue and overwork La Salle fell sick, and delayed the expedition for over a month.

On Christmas Eve 1686, the forty-two pathetic survivors held a solemn Mass in the rude chapel and on Twelfth Night they drank to the King's health, not on the customary French wine, but in cold water. The next day, the 17 men deemed fit to travel bade farewell to the 25 poor souls who were to remain. It was a sad moment for everybody. The voyageurs knew they had only a slim chance of reaching Canada and the people who remained knew that without help their fate was sealed.

When the five horses were loaded with the few scant possessions the men had managed to put together, the party marched through the gates of the fort. Trudging through woods and marshes and along buffalo trails, they continued northwards, now and then meeting friendly native hunters on the way. Heavy rains made travelling difficult and the woods were sometimes so thick that the men had to hew down a passage for the horses. Their shoes, made of raw buffalo hide, hardened in the heat, and hurt their feet so badly that they were obliged to keep soaking the shoes in water. They crossed several rivers on rafts or on canoes made from buffalo hides attached to long poles.

On March 15, they reached the Rivière aux Canots (now Trinity River). La Salle had hidden Indian corn and beans on an earlier voyage, and provisions were running short, so the explorer sent Duhaut; a surgeon named Listot; Nika, the Mohegan hunter, and a few others to locate the cache. The food was spoiled, but on the way back the skillful Nika managed to kill two buffalo.

When La Salle heard of the kill he sent his nephew, the hot-tempered Moranget, to help drag the buffalo back. On his arrival at the scene, Moranget discovered Duhaut and another man roasting the marrow bones and other choice pieces of the meat. By frontier law they were entitled to do this, but Moranget flew into a rage and seized the food. The men seethed with anger. They had never liked Moranget. He had previously insulted the surgeon, who had tended to his wounds and he had once abandoned Duhaut in the forest to find his way as best he could.

That night they plotted their revenge.

When Moranget, Nika, and La Salle's servant were asleep, the conspirators took their axes and hacked the three men to death. With this slaughter, the clouds were closing around La Salle. To preserve their own lives, the murderers knew that he too would have to be killed, so they lurked in the woods to await his approach.

Meanwhile, at the camp six miles away, La Salle became more and more uneasy. At a loss to know why the men had not returned, he asked Joutel whether any plot was afoot. On the morning of March 19 he decided to wait no longer. Leaving Joutel in charge of the camp, he set out to search for the missing men, bringing Father Douay with him. As they plodded on, the sight of two vultures hovering overhead indicated the spot where the buffalo had been killed. To show his presence, La Salle fired a shot in the air.

At the sound of the shot, the conspirators hid themselves in the tall grass. Suspecting nothing, La Salle walked into the open and spied one of the mutineers in the distance. He asked the man where Moranget was, and received an insolent reply. Stepping forward to chastise the impudent fellow, La Salle moved into point-blank range. A shot rang out. La Salle pitched forward dead with a bullet through his brain. The conspirators then crowded around the victim yelling insults at the dead man. They stripped his body and left it to be devoured by wild beasts.

The mutineers did not long enjoy their triumph. At first they plundered all La Salle's possessions – one of them even swaggered around in the explorer's famous scarlet cloak. Before long, however, they were quarreling among themselves and all but two of them ended up killing one another. As for the rest of the expedition, Joutel, Abbé Cavelier, Father Douay, and two others managed to get to the Fort St. Louis on the Illinois in July 1688. For some reason, the Abbé Cavelier kept La Salle's death a secret from Tonty, and from the Governor of New France. It was not until the survivors reached France the following year that the secret of the explorer's murder was revealed.

Whatever his faults, La Salle was a noble and commanding figure. He dreamed great dreams and he had the courage to pursue those dreams in the teeth of disasters that would have discouraged lesser mortals. At the age of 43, while still in the vigor of his manhood, he lost his life in the wilds of Texas at the hands of his own men. What brought him down was his proud and solitary nature which made him hosts of enemies everywhere he went. Among his own followers, he was feared and respected but not loved. Yet when compared with other men of his time, he towers head and shoulders above them all.

LAKE SUPERIOR

L. Itasca

Falls Of St. Anthony

Minnesota R.

Mississippi River

Missouri River

Wisconsin R.

Fox R.

St. Francis Xavier

St. Ignace

Michilimackinac

Mackinac Straits

LAKE HURON

Quebec

Montreal

Lachine

St. Lawrence River

Fort Frontenac

LAKE MICHIGAN

Fort Miami

Fort Detroit

Fort Niagara

LAKE ONTARIO

LAKE ERIE

Chicago Portage

Fort St. Joseph

Illinois R.

Fort St. Louis (Starved Rock)

Fort Crèvecoeur

Wabash River

Ohio River

ATLANTIC OCEAN

Chapter Five

Henry de Tonty

Arkansas River

Red River

Brazos R.

Trinity R.

Colorado R.

Mississippi River

Fort Prudhomme

EXPLORATIONS OF LA SALLE
AND HENRY DE TONTY

LEGEND
••••••• 1st exploration route 1682-84 from Canada
– – – 2nd exploration route 1684-87 from France

Nueces R.

Site of Death

Fort St. Louis (Texas)

Matagorda Bay

GULF OF MEXICO

0   500km

Henry de Tonty was one of the great explorers of North America. Today he is almost forgotten; his exploits overshadowed by those of his friend, Cavelier de La Salle. But Tonty was a hero in his own right. One of his greatest feats was his 10 month trek from Fort St. Louis in Illinois country to the borders of present-day Houston County, Texas. The expedition was not for glory or for money. It was a forlorn attempt to rescue the unfortunate survivors of La Salle's colony in the Texas wilderness.

Tonty was born in Italy about 1650. His father was an Italian nobleman, Lorenzo de Tonty, who took part in a rebellion against his Spanish overlord. When the rebellion collapsed, Lorenzo managed to escape to France with his wife and infant son. The family settled in Paris where two other sons were born. One of the sons, Alphonse de Tonty, also made a name for himself in Canada.

In Paris, the Tonty family were penniless refugees until Lorenzo hit on the famous legacy scheme called "the tontine." The plan was to get people to invest money in the scheme and the last survivor would inherit a fortune. The French government was delighted with the idea because if it worked it would pour money into the King's coffers. Unfortunately, the first "tontine" was a disaster and Lorenzo was thrown into the Bastille prison in 1669, where he languished for 8 years.

At the age of 18, Henry joined the French navy. The young cadet saw plenty of action and acquitted himself well. Then in a battle off the coast of Sicily he had his right hand blown off by a grenade and was taken prisoner for six months. His disability did not hold him back. With a metal hand covered in a glove, he spent three more years in the navy. Later on, when he came to Canada, the native people, who were in awe of his hand, named him "Bras de fer" ("Iron hand").

At the end of the wars, Henry returned to the French court. Without money and with very little schooling, he would have to make his own way as best he could. That same year La Salle happened to be in France looking for men and money for his Mississippi expedition. The opportunity was too good to miss. The two men met and La Salle appointed Tonty to be his lieutenant. The explorer had chosen better than he knew. Of all his followers, the 28-year-old Tonty was to be the most able and most devoted.

Their ship arrived in Canada in September 1678. From the beginning, La Salle was delighted with his new lieutenant. In a letter to France he said "I cannot overstate my joy in having him with me. . . . Perhaps you would not have believed him capable of doing things for which a strong constitution, a knowledge of the country, and the free use of two arms seem absolutely necessary. Nevertheless, his energy and ability make him capable of anything."

Shortly after their arrival, the two men set out for Niagara with men and supplies. A few miles above the falls, at a place now called Cayuga Creek, a large boat was to be built to sail across the Great Lakes. It was Tonty's task to supervise the construction while La Salle was away in Fort Frontenac.

That winter, Tonty had a taste of the hardships that would plague the expedition. To begin with, a boat carrying food and supplies was wrecked by a careless pilot and everything aboard was lost. In the depths of winter, the men set about their back-breaking labor, felling trees and building huts to shelter themselves from the cold and snow. None of them had much heart for the job. Cold and often hungry, they grumbled among themselves and some even plotted to rebel.

As well as having to contend with his own sullen men, Tonty was faced with trouble from the Senecas. The tribe had good reason for anger; Niagara was on their land. It was the key to the Great Lakes and in time it could cut off their trade with the western tribes and thus ruin the whole Iroquois nation. As the new boat began to take shape, rumors spread that the Senecas were going to burn it. In spite of the odds against him, Tonty managed to keep the men at their work and maintain peace with the Senecas.

By spring the *Griffin* was built. On La Salle's return, Tonty was sent to the north shore of Lake Erie to search for some missing fur traders. Setting off in his birch bark canoe, he crossed the lake and arrived in Detroit just two days before the *Griffin* sailed into the straits. His heart must have stirred with pride as the vessel glided smoothly into the calm waters. On her prow was carved the image of a mythical monster – the griffin, and from the deck five cannons pointed over the water. Tonty paddled to the vessel and climbed aboard.

After a stormy voyage, the *Griffin* docked at Michilimackinac, the centre of the western fur trade. At the post, several of La Salle's men were drinking and carousing when they should have been on their way back to Montreal with furs. Others had decamped for Sault Ste. Marie taking a large cargo of furs with them. La Salle sent Tonty to Sault Ste. Marie to round up the men and bring them to the mouth of the St. Mary River on the south shore of Lake Michigan.

Tonty got the men together and set out for the St. Mary River, which La Salle called the Miami. On the way, they ran short of provisions. Tonty and a few others pushed on to join La Salle, and the rest of the men went to hunt for food. It was late November and La Salle was anxious to be on his way, so he sent Tonty back to hurry the stragglers along.

The icy wind pierced through their clothing as Tonty and two companions paddled north. In a few days, the wind turned to a gale, and the resulting waves capsized the frail canoe, forcing the men to seek shelter ashore. They managed to save the canoe, but all the food and supplies were lost in the raging waters of Lake Michigan. To go forward now was impossible, so the trio set their course for the Miami river, with only acorns to sustain them on the three day journey. A few days later the rest of the stragglers arrived.

There was little time to rest at Fort Miami. Winter was closing in and the rivers would soon be frozen. By mid-January the party reached the south bank of the Illinois River, near present-day Peoria, where La Salle decided to build a fort and another ship which would sail down the Mississippi.

Day after day the men scanned the horizon for the *Griffin*. La Salle had sent the ship to Niagara with furs and its return was long overdue. The ship also contained the rigging and other supplies necessary to set the new vessel afloat. The *Griffin* had to be found, or new supplies had to be obtained from Montreal. Leaving Tonty in charge of the new outpost named Fort Crèvecoeur, La Salle set out in search of the missing vessel.

Tonty's men had little stomach for their task. Weary of hardship and hard labor, most of them lost faith in the expedition. The present was dismal and the future looked no better. Rumors had spread that La Salle was bankrupt and might never be able to pay their wages. Under Tonty's prodding, they grudgingly plodded ahead and the new ship began to take shape.

All might have been well if a message had not arrived from La Salle. Tonty was requested to survey a nearby cliff called "Starved Rock," as a possible site for a fort. While he was away on his mission, the men mutineed. In their fury, they burned the fort, stole all the furs, ammunition and provisions they could carry, and threw the remainder in the river. On the site of the unfinished ship they scrawled these words: "Nous sommes tous sauvages" ("We are all savages"). The damage done, all but two of the men deserted and fled into the woods.

The two men carried the bad news to Tonty and he rushed back to salvage what he could from the wreckage. With the abandoned forge and the few tools he found littering the ruined fort, he returned to Starved Rock to await the return of his leader. It was a courageous decision. With three men newly arrived from France and two Recollet priests, he was at the mercy of the local tribes who might resent the newcomers.

The natives proved more trustworthy than the renegade French. Throughout the summer, the six men lived unmolested in the Illinois village and Tonty carried on a little fur-trading. The two priests even found a little hut in the village and began to learn the native language. By day the native people tended their cornfields and in the evening they sat around the wigwam fires, feasting and playing games of chance – unaware of the danger creeping steadily in their direction.

The morning of September 10 was peaceful as usual. As the Frenchman and the Illinois went about their tasks, the two priests, Father Membré and Father Gabriel, wandered into the woods for a religious retreat. Then pandemonium broke out. A young man burst into the village with fateful news: he had seen a large band of Iroquois in full war regalia moving stealthily through the nearby woods. That could mean only one thing – the Iroquois were about to attack the unfortunate Illinois.

The reasons for the Iroquois attack were partly commercial. For years they had controlled the fur-trading in the area. Now the French were infringing on their territory and giving arms to their enemies, the Illinois. Fear of Governor Frontenac kept the Iroquois from attacking the French, but the Illinois were fair game.

Tonty and his men were now in a tight corner, because the Illinois suspected their guests of treason. A few years earlier, the French had signed a peace treaty with the Iroquois. Was it not possible that Tonty was in league with their old enemies? In their rage and panic, some of the young braves shouted for Tonty's head. Other hotheads seized the tools and the oven that had been saved from Fort Crèvecoeur and flung them into the river. When a false rumor reached the camp, that a priest and even La Salle himself had been spotted among the Iroquois, the warriors surrounding the three Frenchmen became more menacing. Betraying no sign of fear (for the native people despised a coward), Tonty offered to join the Illinois in their fight against the enemy.

For the time being, his life was safe. But long could the Illinois hold out against a fierce enemy armed with guns and pistols? In frantic haste, the Illinois gathered the women and children and sent them across the river. Meanwhile, the men sang their war dances and prepared to do battle.

In the morning, the Iroquois emerged from the woods and appeared in massive numbers on the broad prairie, while the unfortunate Illinois prepared themselves to fight to the death. The intrepid Tonty saved the day. Casting his gun to the ground and holding aloft a wampum belt as a sign of peace, he walked forward toward the enemy line. Several guns were immediately aimed in his direction and a young brave rushed forward and stabbed him in the ribs. It seemed that his doom was sealed.

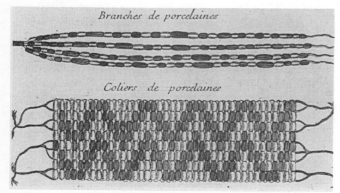

Porcelain strands and a Porcelain Belt.
Reprinted from Bacqueville de la Potherie, C.C. Le Roy. *Historie de l'Amérique septentrionale.* Parie, 1722, vol I. Courtesy National Archives of Canada C 10891.

At that very moment, an Iroquois chief stepped forward. He saw that the man dressed in the native costume was a foreigner, probably a Frenchman. With a word from the chief, Tonty was saved from the jaws of death and taken out of the line of fire. Weak from his wound, he managed to warn the Iroquois that the Illinois were under French protection and could not be attacked without provoking a full-scale war.

The leaders paused to consider what he said. On the one hand it could be dangerous to provoke the French; on the other hand, it was almost impossible to restrain the young braves with the light of battle in their eyes. Skirmishes were already breaking out; one young warrior actually seized Tonty by the hair and thrust a knife toward his neck. With great presence of mind, Tonty told them that there were as many as 50 Frenchmen and 1 000 Illinois warriors in the village.

The ruse worked. Wampum belts were exchanged on both sides and Tonty was allowed to return to the Illinois. As he staggered to his hut, he was assisted by the two Recollet priests who had missed most of the disturbance.

For a while, the Iroquois prowled around the outskirts of the village. When the peace negotiations commenced, an Illinois brave spoiled everything by admitting that they had only 400 men, not the 1 000 that Tonty had claimed. The furious Iroquois called Tonty a liar: "I had much difficulty getting out of that scrape." Fearing another attack, the Illinois abandoned their village and went to join their women and children.

The Iroquois now moved in and took over the plain. In a short while, they had built a fort to protect themselves, and Tonty and his men were inside the walls. Within a week, Tonty was summoned to a council. At the meeting he was presented with several bales of beaver, each one of them having a special meaning. The fifth bale was to indicate that the sky was blue and the sixth was to tell the French that they should be on their way.

The next morning the men left. It was more than six months since they had parted from La Salle at Fort Crèvecoeur and Tonty was impatient for news of his leader. All they could find for their journey was a leaky boat. Setting out in the dangerous craft, they paddled off for Michilimackinac hoping to get there before winter locked the water in its icy grip. At noon on the following day, they went ashore to repair the canoe and set out their wet furs to dry in the sun. Against Tonty's advice, Father Gabriel took a walk into the woods to say his prayers and was never heard from again.

Tonty did his best to find the priest. By day, he and his men searched the woods and in the evening they lit a large fire hoping the old priest would see the smoke. All was to no avail. With heavy hearts they re-embarked, scanning the shoreline in vain for a sight of their old companion. In time, the leaky boat gave out and the men were forced to walk to the Pottawatami village near present-day Green Bay.

The journey was especially hard on Tonty who had not fully recovered from his wound. His legs swollen and in constant pain, he trudged along with nothing to eat except acorns and wild garlic grubbed from under the snow. Near Green Bay they came to an Indian village deserted for the winter. To the wretched men, the few ears of corn and frozen pumpkin they found in the village were welcome finds.

Thus refreshed, they pressed on to the bay, where they were lucky enough to find an abandoned canoe. As they proceeded north on Lake Michigan, fate had another blow in store for them. A violent wind accompanied by driving snow forced them to take shelter on the shore. Despairing of ever reaching the Pottawatomi settlement, they decided to return to the deserted village where, as Tonty says, "we could at least die warm."

On their way back they saw the remains of a fire which temporarily raised their hopes, but when they reached the place they found nobody there. After spending the night by the fire, they woke up to find the water frozen over. There was nothing to be done but to set out again on foot. Their shoes were so tattered that the men had to cut up Father Gabriel's cloak to protect their feet from frostbite. While they toiled away at the makeshift footwear, one of the men became very sick from a piece of rawhide he had eaten to appease his hunger.

The poor man was in such pain that he was unable to travel. As luck would have it, the delay was a blessing in disguise. Two Ottawa warriors happened to see the fire and came to investigate. Taking the famished men in their canoes, the friendly Ottawa took them to the Pottawatami village where they were given a royal feast. "All the Indians seemed to take pleasure in giving us food," wrote Tonty "so that after 34 days of starvation we found our famine turned to abundance."

When spring came, Tonty and his men bade their hospitable hosts good-bye and set out for Michilimackinac. This time the journey was without mishap. To Tonty's great joy, La Salle arrived on the scene shortly after. Now that the men were together, they had many stories of hardships and misfortunes to tell one another. Nevertheless, La Salle was still determined to continue with the expedition.

The party set out again for Fort Frontenac where the two men parted – La Salle to fetch supplies and Tonty to make his way to Fort Miami to assemble some French and native people for the voyage. Toward the end of the year, La Salle joined Tonty and the expedition was finally underway. On April 7, 1682, the sea breezes filled their nostrils and the broad Gulf of Mexico glistened before them. Taking possession of the country in the name of France, La Salle erected a cross on the right bank of the river near present-day Venice, Louisiana. A document attesting to the discovery was drawn up and Tonty was among those who signed it.

The men had to return almost at once in order to replenish their food supply. They paddled upstream, meeting friends and foes on the way, until they came to Fort Prudhomme. Unable to go any further because of a dangerous fever, La Salle sent Tonty ahead to Michilimackinac with orders to send news of the discovery to Quebec. After many narrow escapes from hostile native people he reached his destination in safety.

Part of La Salle's job was completed; however, there was much more to be done. His next step was to build a colony in the Illinois to keep the Iroquois in check and to serve as a fur-trading centre. With this in mind, he sent Tonty down to Illinois country to gather the French who were already in the area and to build a fort. La Salle joined him later in the year, and by spring 1683, the fort was completed and named Fort St. Louis.

Situated on the "Starved Rock" cliff, well protected from possible attack, the new fort overlooked the East Illinois Plains. Both men visited the native tribes and urged them to settle near the post, where they would be protected from the Iroquois. In a few short months the plains were dotted with the lodges of the Illinois who had returned once more to their homeland. In the adjacent prairies and woodlands, several other tribes set up their teepees and placed themselves under the protection of the French. A few Frenchmen also settled nearby on parcels of land granted to them by La Salle.

When La Salle returned to France in September, Tonty was left in charge of the new fort. His tenure was to be short-lived. The new Governor of France, Le Febvre de la Barre hated La Salle and did his best to discredit him in court. As a result, La Barre sent his own friend, Chevalier de Baugy to take over the command of the fort. Tonty bore the blow as best he could, and remained at his post as La Salle's representative. Meanwhile, the Iroquois watched the growing settlement with dismay. To make matters worse, the English traders were urging the natives on to attack the western tribes and drive them out of the Illinois. Tonty and Baugy patched up their differences and prepared for an Iroquois attack. Toward the end of March, the Iroquois converged on the citadel, but after a six day siege, they were driven away.

Shortly afterwards, the tide turned in favor of La Salle. Orders were sent to Governor La Barre that all the explorer's property was to be returned to him. Baugy was recalled to Quebec and Tonty was again in command of Fort St. Louis. With his usual energy, he restored order to the settlement, made peace among warring tribes, and readied for La Salle's long awaited return.

In an effort to find out the cause of the delay, Tonty set off for Michilimackinac. The story there was that the explorer was on his way to the Gulf of Mexico by sea. At his own expense, Tonty gathered an expedition and set off to the aid of his leader. Almost four years to the day after the first discovery, the party arrived at the mouth of the Mississippi, but La Salle was nowhere in sight. After a futile search of the coast, Tonty had to abandon the search. Before leaving, he moved La Salle's original cross, now lying on the sand, to higher ground. Leaving the solitary harbor behind them, the party then turned their canoes for home. A few miles upstream, they were welcomed by a friendly tribe and Tonty gave the chief a letter for La Salle. Fourteen years later, the chief gave the carefully preserved letter to another intrepid Canadian, Le Moyne D'Iberville.

Stopping briefly with various tribes to make alliances with them, Tonty resumed his homeward journey. At the junction of the Arkansas and Mississippi Rivers, there was a tract of land which La Salle had granted to Tonty. Six men received permission to settle on the land and the remainder accompanied Tonty to the Illinois River.

No sooner had Tonty arrived in Fort St. Louis than he was off again — this time to meet the new Governor, Brisay de Denonville. The governor had a plan to strike a blow against the Iroquois from the north, while Tonty would attack them from the rear. Tonty hurried to Fort St. Louis to assemble the native allies for the attack. However, instead of the 600 warriors he had hoped to muster, only 80 were willing to participate in the war. No wonder. If the poor Illinois left their homes, the Senecas were bound to destroy the whole Illinois village.

Eighty men were no match for an Iroquois army. There was nothing to do but to get more men. Leaving a small troop in charge of his fort, Tonty set out for Detroit, where his cousin Dulhut was governor. On their way from Detroit, they captured 60 Englishmen travelling to Michilimackinac. Tonty was very pleased with this coup as it prevented the English from establishing in the west and ruining the French fur trade.

Tonty played his part well in the war with the Iroquis. He led French troops and Indian allies in several battles and helped to build a fort on the Niagara. Denonville's dispatches to France heaped praise on him for his courage and daring.

On his return to Fort St. Louis, Tonty had a surprise awaiting him. La Salle's brother, Abbé Cavelier, and a few compainions who had managed to escape from La Salle's murderers, were in the fort to greet him. In his own words, Tonty welcomed them "as though they had been La Salle himself," and inquired eagerly after his friend. To his shame, Cavelier kept the story of La Salle's murder from the faithful lieutenant. Instead, he told him that the explorer was safe and well in Mexico and he borrowed money from Tonty in La Salle's name.

For two years, from his rock at Fort St. Louis, Tonty continued with his fur-trading, unaware of the the real truth. One day Jean Couture, one of the men who had settled in Arkansas, arrived at the fort and told him the true story. Couture had heard the account from Abbé Cavelier himself, who had visited the Arkansas post on his way home from Texas. It seems that the priest had kept Tonty in the dark to extract money from him.

Tonty was grief-stricken at the loss of his friend. There was nothing he could do for La Salle, but perhaps he could rescue the unhappy colonists abandoned on the shores of Texas. Thus far, not a single person had lifted a hand to help them.

A few months later, Tonty set out for Texas with five Frenchmen and three native people. The first part of the voyage went well. At every Indian village, the party was well received and provided with food and lodging. As the going got rougher, one of the men deserted and two others were killed by the Natchez. Nevertheless, Tonty pushed on. At the borders of present-day Houston County, Texas, he heard word of the lost settlers, but the native people refused to give him guides. Without any ammunition and with only two men left, Tonty was forced to give up.

The long homeward journey was the worst in Tonty's entire career. Torrential rains flooded the land, turning it into a vast bog. The horses they had obtained from the native people became mired in the deep mud and had to be abandoned. Sloshing through water halfway up their legs, the men plodded wearily through the endless marshes. At night they built great piles of tree trunks to protect themselves from the floods. By day they often had to hack their way through dense canes and thick undergrowth. Once the food ran out, they killed and ate two dogs that had followed them from an Indian camp. By the time they managed to reach the little Arkansas settlement, Tonty was ill with a fever. Still weak from his illness, he reached Fort St. Louis in September, after a gruelling 10 month journey.

Tonty was now 40-years-old. During his six years in Canada, he had endured more hardships and dangers than most men would suffer in a lifetime. Beset by famine and disease, winter blasts and summer heats, he had shown remarkable endurance and courage. Back in his Illinois post, he was joined by La Forrest, another friend of La Salle. For a few years he held the fort and continued his fur-trading. In 1691, he had to move close to the present Peoria because the supply of firewood at Fort St. Louis had run out.

At heart, he still dreamt of the Mississippi. In a letter to France he asked the King for money to build a ship which would sail down the Mississippi to France. Like La Salle, he had visions of a southern settlement and a great fur-trading outpost beside a warm water port. In no mood for any further expansion, the court turned down his request.

Another project took form in his fertile brain. If he could not go south, he would travel far into the northwest where the furs were more beautiful and abundant. Year by year, furs were becoming more scarce in the Illinois and it became harder and harder to make a profit. With Frontenac's permission, Tonty set out for Lake Assiniboine in September 1695. How far he went is hard to say, but in June of the following year, he wrote a letter about D'Iberville's capture of Port Nelson on the Hudson Bay.

As a reward for his exploits at Hudson Bay, D'Iberville was chosen to set up a colony at the mouth of the Mississippi. After several years of neglect, the land discovered by La Salle and Tonty was to be settled at last. From his Illinois post, Tonty helped to guide settlers to the new colony. Meanwhile, his own position in Illinois was becoming more and more hopeless. Royal edicts were curbing his trade, furs were becoming scarcer and Tonty was running into debt. In a letter to his brother he complained: "There is no more trade because it is forbidden by the court. . . . All the voyages I have made for the success of the country have ruined me." In 1702, he left Fort St. Louis altogether and made his way to the Mississippi colony.

As usual, Tonty gave loyal service in his new home. He helped to defend the struggling colony and he did his best to keep peace with the native tribes. Two years after his arrival in Louisiana, at the age of 64, he died of a bout of yellow fever.

Little justice has been done to the memory of Henry de Tonty. His name has often been confused with that of his quarrelsome and greedy brother Alphonse. Even his burial place and the exact date and place of his death are unknown. Nevertheless, his bravery and daring entitle him to a place among the great pathfinders of the new world.

LAKE
SUPERIOR

L. Itasca

Quebec

Montreal
Lachine

St. Lawrence River

Falls Of
St. Anthony

Michilimackinac

St. Ignace

LAKE
HURON

LAKE
ONTARIO

Minnesota R.

St.
Francis
Xavier

Mackinac
Straits

Wisconsin R.

Fox R.

Fort
Niagara

Mississippi

Missouri

River

LAKE
MICHIGAN

Fort Detroit

Fort
Miami

LAKE
ERIE

Chicago
Portage

River

Illinois R.

Fort
St. Louis
(Starved
Rock)

Fort
St. Joseph

Fort
Crèvecoeur

Wabash River

Ohio River

Chapter Six

Father Louis Hennepin

Arkansas

River

Red

River

Mississippi

**EXPLORATIONS OF HENNEPIN
1679-80**

Brazos R.

Trinity R.

River

Colorado R.

ATLANTIC

OCEAN

LEGEND

Nueces R.

Matagorda
Bay

GULF OF MEXICO

.... Exploration route with La Salle

– – – – Exploration route of Upper Mississippi

0   500km

Among the explorers of the Mississippi, there is one curious figure, Father Louis Hennepin, a Recollet priest. Dressed in the rough grey robe and sandals of his order, with a rosary and a large crucifix at his waist, Father Hennepin's assignment was to preach the gospel to the native people. In his own mind, he was much more than a preacher; he was a dauntless leader, second only to La Salle himself. When La Salle was dead and unable to contradict him, Hennepin's stories got better and better. He claimed that it was he, not La Salle, who first reached the mouth of the Mississippi. His books full of tall tales and colorful facts became bestsellers all over Europe and Hennepin became an instant success.

Even allowing for his wild exaggerations, Hennepin led a remarkable life. He was born in Ath, Belgium in 1626, the son of a well-to-do merchant. At the age of 17, he entered the Recollet Order and was later ordained a priest. After his ordination, he pestered his superiors to allow him to work in the foreign missions, but they kept him closer to home. For several years, he worked as a preacher around coastal towns such as Calais and Dunkirk, and like other priests in his order, begged alms for the poor. However, he never lost his wanderlust: "I hid my self behind tavern doors while they [the sailors] were talking about their voyages. The tobacco smoke made me dizzy and ill but I did not care. I would have listened whole days and nights, without eating or sleeping, to their stories of the sea and of far away countries."

In 1672, Louis XIV of France invaded the Netherlands and Father Hennepin was assigned to be an army chaplain. By his own account, he endured numerous dangers while caring for the sick and wounded. A few years later, he had welcome news from his superiors. He had been assigned to the missions in New France.

With all the enthusiasm of a much younger man, the 51-year-old Hennepin set forth on his new adventure. On board ship, he got to know Cavelier La Salle who was returning from a visit to France. The over-zealous priest soon locked horns with La Salle. He took it upon himself to scold a party of young women who were dancing and singing to amuse the passengers. La Salle stepped in and told him to mind his own business, which greatly annoyed the meddlesome Hennepin.

On his arrival in Canada, Father Hennepin worked in the missions around Quebec. Travelling on snow shoes or by canoe, he made his way from village to village with his altar strapped to his back, preaching the gospel to the native allies of the French. Shortly afterward, he was sent with another priest to La Salle's settlement at Fort Frontenac. The fort was on the land of the Iroquois, who had little love for the French or their religion. Undeterred, Father Hennepin went to work. He had a mission house with a huge cross erected at the fort and he began to preach to the native people.

His love of adventure and his zeal for souls took him on treks deep into Iroquois territory. On these excursions, he learned the language and translated some of the Catholic prayers for the children. He sampled and enjoyed the native food - wild rice, sagamite, bear meat, squirrels and many other dishes. Once, however, the Mohawks offered him a dish of frogs mixed with meal which was not at all to his liking.

When La Salle returned from France in 1678, Hennepin was in Quebec to meet him. The explorer's news was music to the ears of the priest. La Salle's voyage to the Mississippi would soon begin and Father Hennepin was to be one of the party. Carrying with him his portable altar, a mat and a blanket, he set off for Fort Frontenac in a birch bark canoe paddled by two men. On the way he stopped off now and then to say Mass and preach the gospel in the small settlements along the St. Lawrence.

Early in November, he joined his Recollet friends in Fort Frontenac. From there a contingent under Lussier La Motte were to travel ahead of La Salle to Niagara to start work on a fort. Five miles below Niagara Falls at what is now La Salle, New York the men commenced work on Fort Conti. The Seneca Indians grumbled among themselves they did not want a French fort on their land.

To try to placate the Senecas, La Motte took Hennepin and a few other men to the great Seneca native village, near present-day Rochester, New York. The native people received their visitors very well. "The young men washed our feet," remembered Hennepin, "and rubbed them all over with oil and grease." In their speech the chiefs were "as grave and dignified as Italian senators." In spite of the good reception, the chiefs refused to make any promises of friendship.

Throughout the winter, while the men constructed a ship above the falls, Hennepin preached and said Mass in a little rude chapel. He also scribbled away in his notebook, which, he says, made Tonty jealous. In spring, Hennepin returned to Fort Frontenac to fetch two other Recollet priests who were also to join the expedition.

Before he left Niagara, he had a chance to get a good look at the falls. In his eyes, they were a terrifying sight: "It is so rapid above the descent, that it violently hurries down the wild beasts trying to pass to feed on the other side, casting them headlong above five hundred feet. . . . " His description of the falls is the first written one we have.

Hennepin continued with La Salle's expedition as far as Fort Crèvecoeur, near present-day Lake Peoria, Illinois. On one canoe ride, the hardy man showed his metal. A violent storm lashed Lake Michigan, forcing the men to wade to shore and Hennepin carried the 65-year-old Father Gabriel on his back to safety. As the men toiled away at the fort, he kept an eye on everything and gave out unwanted advice. Since they were out of wine, he was unable to say Mass, but he made up for this by preaching long sermons every morning and evening. Whether the surly men appreciated his contribution is another question. In any event, La Salle soon had another mission for Hennepin. With Michael Accau and Picard Du Guay, he was sent off to explore the Illinois River and the upper reaches of the Mississippi.

On February 29, the three men set out on their voyage of discovery, their canoe laden with knives, awls, tobacco and other gifts for the natives. It seems that Accau was in charge of the project and Hennepin's job was to preach the gospel to any tribes they might meet on the way. From the day of their departure until the coureur de bois, Greysalon Duluth rescued them in July, we have only Hennepin's word for what transpired. He wrote two books about his experiences, each of them telling a different story. In his first book, he tells of his experiences on the route mapped out for him by La Salle. According to the second book published many years later, he and his two companions actually paddled to the mouth of the Mississippi. This would be a total journey of over 3 000 miles in little over a month, if all the stops he mentions are taken into account.

From other evidence about the places and people he met, the first account seems to be reasonably accurate. Of course, he would not be Father Hennepin if he didn't boast about his exploits and make himself appear to be the real leader of the expedition. Bearing these points in mind, we can now follow the trio on their way.

They paddled down the river without mishap until they reached the Mississippi junction, where they were delayed for a few days by floating ice. Turning north, they plied their oars against the currents of the

Upper Mississippi, their eyes searching for any sign of Sioux warriors. On April 12, somewhere in present-day Wisconsin, their boat sprang a leak. Hennepin busied himself repairing the leak, while his two companions lit a fire and began roasting a wild turkey.

Sioux Indian
© British Library Photo Service.

Suddenly the peaceful scene was shattered; a flotilla of canoes bearing over 100 shouting warriors was bearing down on the hapless trio. The men's worst fears were soon realized. They were surrounded by the dreaded Sioux in full war regalia.

All might have been well if Hennepin had kept his head. One of the chiefs shouted out the word "Miamiba" which Hennepin rightly understood to be "Miami." The Sioux were obviously on the warpath in search of their enemies, the Miamis. With his stick, the priest drew a rough map indicating that the Miami were far away on the other side of the river. Since the warriors saw they had no hope of catching up with their enemies, they seized the Frenchmen instead.

From then on, the Sioux played a cat and mouse game with their captives. Holding up their warclubs as a warning, they forced the men to give up their food and possessions. Then the three men were made to land their canoe on the opposite shore where the whole party camped for the night. There was little sleep for the three captives, expecting, as they did, to be murdered in their beds.

At dawn a young chief approached the three frightened travellers. With the use of signs, he indicated that they were to return with the Sioux to their village. Glad to be spared, Father Hennepin shortly took out his breviary and began muttering his prayers. At this, the warriors angrily encircled him, for they thought he was trying to cast a spell on the company. Not unnaturally, Accau and Du Guay begged the priest to desist, but the stubborn Hennepin continued to do what he thought as his duty. Before the wrath of the natives descended on his head, he thought of a clever ruse. He stopped his muttering and began to chant the prayers in a loud, cheerful voice. This appeased the Sioux, who liked chanting.

For several days, the Sioux and their three captives continued their journey. Every morning they arose at the crack of dawn and paddled upstream, stopping now and then to hunt for food. At night the Frenchmen slept beside a young chief, who was friendlier than his companions. However, Hennepin reported that one incident scared him half to death. After killing a bear, the warriors painted their bodies, donned their feathers and began to dance a war dance, while the chief placed his hands on the heads of the three Frenchmen. Father Hennepin expected the worst, but the dance concluded and no life was taken.

Near present-day St. Paul, Minnesota, he had cause for further alarm. Heading for the shore, the men beached their canoes and smashed the French boat to pieces. All the French possessions were then divided among members of the different tribes. What particularly galled Father Hennepin was the sight of his beautiful gold vestments in the hands of the natives.

The distribution over, the party proceeded on foot to their homeland. It was a gruelling trek. Poor Hennepin was not a young man and he was unable to keep up with the fleet-footed Sioux. He was so slow that at times the Indians burned the grass behind him to make him walk faster. At other times, he was forced to plunge into cold streams and swim to the other side. Nevertheless, he endured no worse than anyone else. They all shared the same food and put up with the same hardships.

Exhausted and half-starved, the motley crew arrived at a Sioux village never previously penetrated by white men. On their arrival, everyone sat down to a tasty meal of wild rice mixed with berries, after which the three companions were parted. Poor Hennepin trembled with dismay when he found himself assigned to an old chief who had always shown a hearty dislike for the priest.

However, his fears were unfounded. The old chief adopted him as his son and brought him safely to his own village. In the chief's lodge, Hennepin was allowed to sit down on a bearskin and a young boy rubbed his bones with the fat of a wildcat. A few times a week they gave him one of their sweat baths to relieve his aches and pains. For his part, Hennepin did his best to keep in their good graces. He shaved the heads of the children, looked after them when they were sick and amazed them with the workings of his compass.

In a short time, the whole band, with Hennepin in tow, set out on a buffalo hunt. When they reached the river bank no one was anxious to take him aboard a canoe. Even his two companions, who were also in the group, turned their backs on him. The poor priest was in a quandary. At any moment the flotilla could set out, leaving him to fend for himself. Fortunately for him, two warriors took pity on him and took him aboard.

Sioux Indian with child
© British Museum Photo Service

After reaching the Mississippi, the party set up their camp on a nearby hill. The Sioux were probably tired of the Frenchmen. A novelty at first to people who were not acquainted with white men, the captives had become a nuisance, eating up the scarce food that the Sioux needed for themselves. At his request, Hennepin was allowed to take a boat and Du Guay offered to go with him. The two men struck out toward the Wisconsin River, leaving Accau behind because he preferred to stay with the Sioux. As they paddled along, Hennepin discovered the waterfall which he named "The Falls of St. Anthony." On they went down the glassy river, living on game and turtles. Once they also succeeded in killing a buffalo and ate so well that they were sick for two days. They even managed to rig up a fishing line, which they used to snare amazingly large cat fish.

Near Lake Pepin, they met a Sioux hunting party which included their companion Accau. They decided to join the party. In the course of the hunt, Hennepin was separated from his companions and was forced to travel in a battered canoe paddled by an old woman. The priest was cut to the quick. To his annoyance, he was put to work bailing the water from the canoe with a bark dish, while the 80-year-old woman handled the boat and kept three small children in order.

After the hunt, on their way upstream, the French were rescued at last. By good luck, Tonty's cousin, Greysalon Dulhut, happened to be exploring in the area and heard that there were some Europeans on the river. With five men, he sped down the river to the rescue. At the sight of Dulhut, the Sioux turned friendly, for they had heard of him from their northern cousins. A great feast was prepared in Dulhut's honor and Father Hennepin was treated with a lot more respect than before. On their departure the old chief even drew them a map to guide them on their journey home to Canada.

Father Hennepin among the Sioux.

Father Hennepin's Canadian troubles were now behind him. Leaving Sioux country, the party paddled to Green Bay and from there to Michilimackinac, where Father Hennepin spent the winter with the Jesuits. The stalwart priest was none the worse for his ordeal. To while away his time, he often went skating and ice fishing with one of the Jesuit priests. By summer he was back in Montreal. Looking out his window one day, Frontenac saw a man walking by in a tattered grey robe patched with buffalo skins. The man was Hennepin. As soon as he recognized him, the Governor invited him into his house where the priest no doubt regaled him with the stories of his adventures.

The following year Hennepin was back in France busily writing a book about his experiences. The book, later translated into several languages, was a huge success and Hennepin became a celebrity. With fame came new positions of authority in the Recollet order. Unfortunately, he soon fell from grace. Quarrelsome as ever, he found himself at loggerheads, not just with his superiors, but with outsiders as well.

Still undaunted, he tried to get the King of England interested in his discoveries, but the King didn't want any clashes with France. Needless to say, his offer to England did not endear Hennepin to King Louis XIV of France.

Out of favor with almost everyone, Father Hennepin had another trick up his sleeve. His weapon was his pen. In 1698, he wrote a new book. In this new volume, full of tall stories of his own and details gleaned from the diary of Father Membré, he claimed that he and his two companions had managed to go to the mouth of the Mississippi and back before being captured by the Sioux. According to Hennepin, he had kept quiet about the voyage so as not to offend La Salle. Full of contradictions though it was, the book was an immense success. Avid for stories about the strange new land, most Europeans, who knew nothing about places or distances in North America, were completely hoodwinked.

Knowledgeable people distrusted his stories or called him an out and out liar. "I do not know how Father Hennepin had the boldness to lie so impudently," wrote Tonty. "He was insupportable to the late M. de Salle and to all of La Salle's men." A priest talked about the publication as "that wretched book" that enraged him so much. Nevertheless, the book continued to sell.

He even found time to write a third book mainly about La Salle's voyage to Texas. Meanwhile, he still hankered to return to Canada. When he was 70-years-old he made a plea to that effect to the French ambassador to Holland. For a time it looked as if his request might succeed, mainly to get him out of the way, but King Louis put his foot down. His orders were to have Hennepin arrested if he ever set foot in the colony. Father Dollier de Casson, the superior of the Sulpicians, wrote jokingly to the head of the Recollet friars asking them not to send another Father Louis to Canada if the two orders were to live in peace with one another.

As a last resort, Father Hennepin went to Rome where he stirred up more trouble. In a few years he was back in Holland and he died there in 1705.

Poor Hennepin brought most of his troubles on himself. Not content with his own laurels, he tried to snatch the crown from others, including La Salle. In his second book, he even claimed that Louis Jolliet was a fraud, who had never found the Mississippi. A tough energetic man, Hennepin deserves his share of glory. He discovered the Falls of St. Anthony and he was one of the first people to live among the Sioux. However, in the end, his vanity was his undoing.

Algonkians

A large number of tribes who lived in the eastern part of Canada from Ontario to the Atlantic Coast. They all spoke dialects of the same language (Algonkian) and lived almost entirely on hunting and fishing.

Algonkin

One of the largest tribes of the Algonkian family, after whom both the language and the whole group of tribes are named.

Bull Boat

A boat made by stretching skins over a wooden frame shaped like a circular basket. The boat was used by the prairie Indians.

Cache

A hiding place where food and other goods were hidden for safekeeping.

Calumet

A pipe used to burn tobacco as an offering to the Great Spirit and as a sign of friendship. The calumet was also a symbol of tribal power and unity. It had a long shaft painted in different colors and adorned with quills, heads, fur and feathers. The bowl was carved from stone or clay often engraved with designs.

Company of One Hundred Associates (Compagnie Des Cent Associés)

An organization of merchants and noblemen founded in 1627. A French law conferred the whole of the North American continent on the company and gave its members a monopoly on the fur trade. In return, the Associates promised to send 300 people to Canada each year, to support the settlers for three years and to provide each community with priests. The Company was dissolved in 1663.

Coureurs de Bois – Unlicensed Fur Traders of New France

Despite repeated warnings from the government, these renegades traded freely with the native people and played an important role in exploration and in establishing contact with the nature people

Donné

A lay helper who sometimes accompanied priests on their missions.

Five Nations

See Iroquois.

Habitation – Settlement

The name is usually given to the group of houses constructed to shelter and protect the first settlers, e.g., the habitations at Port Royal and Quebec.

Hurons

A group of tribes which broke away from the Iroquoian community. A great trading nation, they acted as middlemen between the French and the northern tribes. Generally allied to the French, the Huron nation was destroyed by the Iroquois in 1650.

Illinois

the Illinios-Miami tribes lived in the Mississippi valley around the present state of Illinois.

Intendant

The most important administrative officer in New France, eventually responsible for the administration of finance, justice and police in the colony.

Iroquois

(*Also known as the* Five Nations *and after they were joined by the* Tuscaroras *in 1722, the* Six Nations.

A league of five nations – the Mohawks, the Oneidas, the Onondagas, the Cayugas and the Senecas. They lived mainly in the present state of New York. The Hurons, the Tobacco Naiton, and the New Tribes, all of who lived in southern Ontario, were also Iroquoian tribes, but they did not belong to the league.

Pemmican

Dried meat, usually bison, beaten into coarse powder and mixed with melted fat and sometimes berries. The pemmican was cooled and packed in bison hide bags which could be carried long distances.

Peorias

One of the Illinois tribes.

Portage

A land route around an interruption in a waterway. When travellers were unable to continue on their journey by canoe, they hoisted their goods and canoes on their backs and continued until they reached the next section of navigable water where they re-launched their boats.

Potlatch

A large celebration among the west coast Indian tribes, where wealth such as blankets, cedar boxes, fish, canoes and even slaves, were bestowed on others, or even ceremonially destroyed. On such occasions chiefs tried to outdo each other in generosity. Potlatches were held to honor new chiefs, to mourn the dead, and to mark other important occasions, and a great potlatch could last for days and even weeks.

Sachem

An Algonkian word meaning "chief".

Sagamite

A thin porridge made of husked corn mixed with fish, berries and/or whatever edibles were available.

Sagamo

See "Sachem."

Seigneurial System

Modeled after the French feudal system, it was started in the hope that the owner of a large grant of land would bring our settlers from France to cultivate the soil and make their homes in New France. The seigneur paid nothing for the land and settlers paid a small rent and worked six days each year for their masters.

Six Nations

See Iroquois.

Travois

A transportation device among the Plains Indians. It was made of two long poles with a framework at the back to hold baggage. The poles were lashed to the pike, a dog or a horse.

Voyageur

The name generally given to adventurous men who travelled by canoe into the interior of the country to trade with the native people.

Wampum

Originally made of white and purple sea shells and later of beads strung together into strings, belts and sashes. It was used by the Indians as money, oraments and ceremonial pledges. It was also used in the fur trade as a means of exchange. Wampum belts with particular patterns were used to cement treaties and on other important occasions. The designs in the wampum helped the native people to remember past events.

Selected Bibliography

Campbell, T. J. *Pioneer Priests of North America*. Vols. 2 and 3. New York: The America Press, 1911.

Charlevoix, Francis Xavier. *History and General Descriptions of New France*. Translated with notes by J. G. Shea. Chicago: Loyola University Press, 1744.

Gox, Isaac Joslin. *The Journeys of Réné Robert Cavelier, Sieur de La Salle*. New York: Allerton, 1922.

Eccles, W. J. *Frontenac, the Courtier Govenor*. Toronto: McClelland and Stewart, 1959.

Gagnon, Fredrick Ernest. *Louis Jolliet*. Montreal: Beauchemin, 1913.

Grandbois, Alain. *Born in Quebec* Translated by Evelyn M. Brown. Montreal: Palm, 1964.

Hamilton, Raphael. *Marquette's Explorations*. Madison, Wisconsin: University of Wisconsin Press, 1970.

Havighorst, Walter. *Three Flags at the Straits*. Englewood Cliffs, New Jersey: Prentice Hall, 1966.

The Jesuit Relations and Allied Documents. Edited and translated by R. G. Thwaites. New York: Pageant Books, 1959.

Parkman, Francis. *La Salle and the Discovery of the West*. Boston: Little Brown, 1879.

Repplier, Agnes. *Père Marquette*. Garden City, New York: Doubleday, 1929.

Severin, Timothy. *Explorers of the Mississippi*. New York: Knopf, 1968.